SUCCESS UNLIMITED

WITH

ADDA HAFBORG

Proven Strategies from Today's
Leading Experts

Also Featuring
Best-Selling Author Matt Morris
and
Other Top Authors

© 2018 Success Publishing

Success Publishing, LLC
2810 Trinity Mills, #209-221
Carrollton, Texas USA 75006

All rights reserved. No part of this book may be reproduced, stored in a retrieval system, or transmitted in any form or by any means - electronic or mechanical, photocopy, recording, or any other - except for brief quotations in printed reviews, without the prior permission of the publisher. Although the author(s) and publisher have made every effort to ensure the accuracy and completeness of information contained in this book, we assume no responsibility for errors, inaccuracies, omissions, or any inconsistency herein.

ISBN-13: 978-1-7326353-3-3 (Paperback)

Table of Contents

CHAPTER 1
Fear And Self-Doubt To Feeling Good In My Own Body
By Adda Hafborg 5

CHAPTER 2
The Power Of Manifestation
By Matt Morris.. 19

CHAPTER 3
Key To Success Is focus
By Jason Reid 29

CHAPTER 4
How To Work Less, Earn More And Live Free As A Lifestyle Entrepreneur
By Francis Ablola 41

CHAPTER 5
Your Partner In Crime: The Subconscious Mind
By Oliver T. Asaah.. 55

CHAPTER 6
The Journey Of Success
By Dr. Steven & Dr. Terresa Balestracci... 71

CHAPTER 7
25 Birthday Cakes
By Blake Fleischacker 85

CHAPTER 8
Essential Success "A Living Transformation"
By Ray Blanchard, Ph.D. 97

CHAPTER 9
Journey To "Success"
By Crystal Wolfchild 113

CHAPTER 10
Reaching Success With Excellence
By Ellen Reid 125

CHAPTER 11
Becoming The Man In The Arena
By Mikel Erdman 135

CHAPTER 12
Engineer Your Success
By Julie Eversole 153

CHAPTER 13
Bouncing Back Successfully from Any Circumstance
By Henry Maltez 167

CHAPTER 14
Living Intrepidly
By Demi Karpouzos 183

CHAPTER 15
Inspiration When You Least Expect It
By Brian Mahany 193

CHAPTER 16
The Money Line
By Marc Accetta 207

CHAPTER 17
What Legacy Are You Going To Leave Behind?
By Jill Nieman Picerno 221

Chapter 1
FEAR AND SELF-DOUBT TO FEELING GOOD IN MY OWN BODY

By Adda Hafborg

"The more we hide our feelings, the more they show. The more we deny our feelings, the more they grow." - Unknown

Here is a gift from me to you. My story can hopefully help someone in the journey from fear and self-doubt to feeling good in their own body and mind. I lived a good, safe life in Iceland with my hubby, my teenage daughter and our three dogs in a beautiful modern house with two cars. Both of us had good jobs.

But, I have always known that I am not an ordinary woman who is satisfied with living life without action and adventure. I didn't want to listen to my inner self for many years, because from the outside, everything looked good and I felt okay. But, something was missing in my life.

Deep down in my heart, I desired more freedom to travel the world, learn about other countries and get to know more people and their cultures. One cold day in November 2011, our friends came over, and they wanted us to work with them on network marketing.

For three years, people all around me had tried to recruit me into this "thing," but I had tried network marketing twice in the past, and I was never going to do it again. The strange thing is that whenever I say to myself "never again," the opposite seems to happen. I am very polite, so I said "yes" when they showed us the presentation, but after that, I said a BIG "NO, THANK YOU." When they were leaving, one of our friends said these golden words to me "Adda, it is ok to change your mind." That night, I could not sleep; my mind was on fire.

"This is good; this is something for me, I can do this." After three days, I called one of our friends and asked, "Can you guys sign me in, please?" After one year of all kinds of struggles and victories, I decided to go all in, and I quit my corporate job. People around me were skeptical and asked, "Are you really going to quit a very good job for this pyramid thing?" I said 'yes' with pride, but deep inside, I was scared. "What if this is not going to work for me?" My fear and self-doubt started to kick in, but with positive self-talk and reading books about personal development, I kept on going. My hubby and I made a contract with each other before quitting my job. If my salary in our network marketing company did not at least double in six months, I would look for another job. I was unstoppable. I did not want to look for another job. I loved the people and the freedom in network marketing.

I had made my decision... My eyes glowed with positive energy. "Let's do this," I said. My mind was full of faith; I believed in myself, the company and my team. The growth started to be unbelievably fantastic. For two and a half years, we had great MOMENTUM, and we started to build businesses in other countries as well.

The internet is a great tool to build businesses worldwide. My team was growing fast. I started to travel the world to support my team, and I loved it. I am so grateful for all the great friendships I have built with fantastic people all over the world because of network marketing. I have friends in Iceland, Holland, Michigan, Minnesota, Denmark, Norway, Sweden, Finland, Spain, Germany, Latvia, Estonia and many more.

Then during the summer of 2015, life happened to me. I had self-doubt to the point that I was making my decisions based on what other people were saying about me behind my back, not what I knew was the truth about myself. I was constantly struggling with confidence and always second-guessing myself. What I've learned from my experiences is that I need to feed my mind with positivity every single day. I need to surround myself with positive people who think of solutions like me.

All of us have good and bad days in our lives. I truly believe that if I let go of other people's opinions and listen to my own positive voice every single day, I can find a positive daily balance. I've found out a few things that help a lot with my self-doubt and confidence; these may help you too:

1. Stop comparing my accomplishments to that of my friends and colleagues.

I find that I doubt myself the most when I'm comparing what I'm doing with what other people are doing. When I compare my accomplishments to a colleague, I start feeling inadequate. My colleague's accomplishments are not a litmus test for my success. One key thing to remember when we find ourselves in this mental pattern is that everyone is on his or her own journey. I find that I am most successful in my personal and professional life when I am following what works for me and what makes me feel good, even if it is different from what the people I look up to are doing.

2. Forget about what everyone is thinking about me.

When we care about what everyone else is thinking about us, we inhibit ourselves. We often would rather do nothing and not get judged than do something and risk being criticized. Worrying about what other people think of us will continue to hold us back from doing some great things.

3. Accept that my fears and doubts are within me, and I need to give them room, and not try to escape them.

Whatever thoughts and feelings come up inside of me, I'll be ok with them. Stop resisting what I feel and think. Avoidance is not the answer. Even though fear and doubt are painful, they are not the problem; my reaction to them is. Problems arise when we try to get rid of, hide or control our self-doubt and fear. When we start accepting how we feel and think in any given moment, we start noticing that feelings and thoughts are like the clouds in the sky; they are just passing by.

Whenever I feel the urge not to take action, I remind myself to act on what I truly desire: making meaningful connections and enjoying life to the fullest.

4. I believe pure gratitude from our hearts is a powerful help in every situation in our lives.

In a study by McCraty and colleagues (1998), 45 adults were taught to "cultivate appreciation and other positive emotions." The results of this study showed that there was a mean 23% reduction in the stress hormone cortisol after the intervention period.

Moreover, during the use of the techniques, 80% of the participants exhibited an increased coherence in heart rate variability patterns, indicating reduced stress. In other words, these findings suggest that people with an "attitude of gratitude" experience lower levels of stress.

In another study by Seligman, Steen, and Peterson (2005), participants were given one week to write and then deliver a letter of thanks in person to someone who had been especially kind to them, but who had never been properly thanked.

The gratitude visit involves three basic steps:

First, think of someone who has done something important and wonderful for you, yet who you feel you have not properly thanked.

Next, reflect on the benefits you received from this person, and write a letter, expressing your gratitude for all they have done for you.

Finally, arrange to deliver the letter personally, and spend some time with this person talking about what you wrote.

The results showed that participants who engaged in the letter-writing exercise reported more happiness for one month after the intervention compared to a control group. Expressing gratitude not only helps us to appreciate what we received in life; it also helps us to feel that we've given something back to those who helped us.

5. Read positive books every day.

One of the best ways to boost my confidence is to listen to or read some of my favorite self-development books.

My favorite sources are:
- The Magic Of Thinking Big by David J. Schwartz
- The Greatest Networker In The World by John M. Fogg
- The Seasons Of Life by Jim Rohn
- Think And Grow Rich by Napoleon Hill

I put the audiobooks on my iPhone and listen to them whenever I'm walking, driving or chilling at the beach. I also spend quiet time on my balcony with a book.

6. Write in a gratitude journal at the beginning of each day.

It is so easy to focus on what we don't have rather than what we do have. Giving those feelings energy will only create more situations which I don't like to have in my life.

Instead of focusing on what I am lacking, I like to focus on what I have and what I have accomplished. Feelings of gratitude put us in a positive frame of mind. When we're feeling positive, we're feeling good. And when we're feeling good, good things happen.

7. When my decisions were made back then, I had many negative thoughts, my self-doubt took over, and I often gave up even before I started.

Mel Robbins' tips. "The 5-second rule," has changed my life. When I count 5-4-3-2-1 go... I just do the things I planned to do, and it feels good.

Okay, back to my story. All our five children had started their own lives; my husband and I were in our big house (with our dogs). That Fall of 2015, my hubby and I got divorced, and I moved out. I felt miserable. Few people knew that because I was always smiling, but in my eyes and in my heart, there was no joy. I kept on doing my network marketing business, but it was not easy. In one year, I lost about half of my team members. I was depressed and felt sorry for myself. "Poor, miserable me."

But one day, when the smell of the spring passed through my window, I decided that "Ok, Adda, now is the time for you to find your 'big girl shoes' and stop this negative nonsense." I remembered that somewhere in my notes, I had three great questions from the Dale Carnegie training that I had once used before at a difficult moment in my life.

Here are the three questions. It is very important to write down the answers honestly.

1. What is the worst thing that can happen?

2. What is the possible thing to do about it?

3. What am I going to do about it?

These questions helped me to focus on what I really want in life and to follow my dreams with a positive attitude. In July 2016, I decided to move to Spain. One of my best friends invited me to rent a room in her apartment near Torrevieja and see if I would like to build my own home in Spain one day.

It's been over two years now, and I am building up a fantastic life with my fiancé in a beautiful little town in southern Spain. I can go to Iceland to be with my grandchildren and my family, and they also come to Spain. The world is not so big after all. My network marketing business is growing again, and I am not scared of the future anymore.

It is up to me to accept my fear and self-doubt and put up a positive exception to every situation so that I can be the best version of myself on a daily basis. I believe that what we feed our brain daily is the foundation of our future. Hope you all are having a great day today, just like every other day.

Biography

Adda Hafborg is an Entrepreneur, Mentor, and Influencer. She has built her leaders' organization in 13 different countries. Her strength is her positive long-term vision. She influences others to reach their goals and find balance in life while she leads by example.

Contact Information

Facebook
https://www.facebook.com/arny.halfdansdottir#!/arny.halfdansdottir
YouTube
https://www.youtube.com/channel/UCeR16SV7vlekxEnbBMplwfw
Instagram https://www.instagram.com/addahafborg/

Chapter 2
THE POWER OF MANIFESTATION

By Matt Morris

It had been about three days since my last bath. Not that you could even call it a bath. Every two or three days, I would find a gas station bathroom that would lock from the inside. I'd take off all my clothes, splash water up from the sink, soap up, and then splash water to rinse off. I remember always praying that no one would be waiting outside because the floor would be soaking wet.

I had completely run out of money. I had also run out of credit. I was approximately $30,000 in debt and couldn't even make the minimum payments on my credit cards. I had been forced to live out of my car because I couldn't afford rent or even $20 a night to stay in a sleazy motel. I was selling above ground swimming pools in southern Louisiana during the two hottest months of the year and didn't get paid commissions until the pool got installed six to eight weeks later. So, for two months, my Honda Civic was my home sweet home.

Sitting all alone in my car that night, I was overly aware that my life had hit rock bottom. Not only was I lonely, broke and living out of my car, but I had just showered naked in the rain in the church parking lot in which I was parked. To be specific, I had showered under the gutter runoff from the roof of the church.

The burning question in my mind that night was, "How?" How in the world had I gotten myself into this situation? I knew I wasn't there because of a lack of effort or even a lack of intelligence. (I wasn't lazy, and I actually considered myself to be a pretty smart guy.)

After experiencing both utter failure and extreme success in my life, I have become acutely aware of what exactly manifested that situation. I'm also aware of what has now allowed me to become a self-made millionaire, travel around the world to over 50 countries, become a best-selling author and speaker attracting audiences of thousands every year.

You might think what caused those results were the *actions* leading up to them because, as we know, every action does produce a result. Most people focus only on the "how to's" but never seem to achieve their full potential because the decision to take proper or improper actions is a byproduct of your original intention. If the intention is not set properly, one will almost always make the wrong decisions on what actions to take which, in turn, lead to an undesired result.

What lies at the heart of manifesting your full potential is your intention.

What is intention? The dictionary defines it as the end or objective intended or purpose. While that sounds incredibly simple, utilizing the power of intention needs a bit more clarification of how you truly manifest that purpose for yourself.

An intention is your inner belief of what is already present but has simply not manifested in physical form yet. A true intention comes with the commitment and honest belief that anything else is an absolute impossibility. You see, when you're committed to a result, it's already done. Without it already being done in your mind, it cannot be considered a true intention but simply a fleeting wish.

When it comes to achieving your result, the simplest and widely accepted model for you to follow is what we call *cause and effect*. Think of your result as your effect. Your job is to identify and create the cause that will produce your effect.

Most people naturally assume that the cause is the physical actions or the steps you need to take to get your desired effect. What I'm proposing to you here, however, is that the series of action steps is not the real cause. The actions are really part of the effect.

So, the question is then, what's the cause?

The real cause is the intention you made to create that effect in the first place. The moment you say to yourself, "let it be so," is the real cause. Without the decision or your intention, the effect will never manifest. Your intention is ultimately what causes everything in your life to manifest.

If you want to achieve a goal, the most crucial part is to *decide* to manifest it. It doesn't matter if you feel it's out of your capabilities to achieve it. It doesn't matter if you can't see *how* you're going to achieve it. The *how* is insignificant because the universe will usually never manifest the *how* until *after* you've made the decision.

If you look at the origin of the word "decide," it is actually "to cut off." Your "decision" then should be framed in your mind as cutting off any other option other than your desired result. If failure is an option in your mind, your true intention is actually failure.

So step 1 is to *decide* not to wonder if you can do it and not to think of all the reasons that are holding you back. If you want to start your own business, then decide to make it so first. If you want to get married, decide to attract a mate. Whatever it is you want out of life, make a decision and a commitment *first,* and *then* work out the *how.*

If you have doubts in your head, you will find doubts in the world. You see, my belief is that the universe can sense a lack of commitment to a goal. It's like those people who say they are going to *try* to do something and *see how it goes.* When you come from a place of uncertainty or if you're wishy-washy about your goal, then the universe is not going to help you achieve it.

When you have total certainty in declaring your intention, you attract people like a magnet. When you are energized, motivated and have declared your goal to be so, that resonates in your being, and the universe aligns itself to work with you to manifest your intention.

You must also realize that your subconscious mind is infinitely more powerful than your conscious mind and that your subconscious mind controls your outcome 100%. When you are uncertain consciously about your goal, your subconscious does everything in its power to hold you back. You see, your subconscious acts like a computer. It accepts 100% of the data your conscious mind gives it. When your conscious mind feeds it negativity, it produces negative results for you. When your conscious mind feeds it excitement, positivity, and certainty, it produces all the energy and creativity it possibly can to ensure that you accomplish your intended result.

If you want to achieve any goal, your first step is to declare it and then to clear out all words like "hopefully," "can't," "maybe" and the killer - "try." When someone tells me they're going to "try" to do something, I know that they're *not* going to do it.

Such words are all signs of a lack of commitment, that you don't believe in yourself and that you're using your own power against yourself. You see, we all have the same amount of power – it's just deciding if we want to use our power negatively or positively. When you use your power negatively, you're saying, "let me be powerless." If you think weakness, you manifest weakness. If you project certainty, you manifest certainty.

"Energy flows where attention goes."

You get whatever you think about most often. Whatever you think about expands. Therefore, we must constantly focus on what we want!

Remember, "we" create our destiny by the committed focus of our intention.

Biography

Author of the International Bestselling *The Unemployed Millionaire*, Matt Morris began as a serial entrepreneur at 18. Since then, he has generated over $1.5 billion through his sales organizations totaling over one million customers worldwide. As a self-made millionaire and one of the top Internet and Network Marketing experts, he's been featured on international radio, television and spoken from platforms to audiences in over 25 countries around the world. And now, as the founder of Success Publishing, he co-authors with leading experts from every walk of life.

http://www.MattMorris.com | http://successpublishing.com/

Chapter 3
KEY TO SUCCESS IS FOCUS

By Jason Reid

"Success is finding within yourself the ability to leave everyday, thing, and person better than you found them. And be happy doing it." - Jason Reid

I remember being all scrunched up over an actual non-electronic tablet, the old paper kind, with a pencil, writing the table of contents for my new "bestseller." I was probably about eleven years of age. I'm pretty sure it got thrown out a few years later, and I can't remember if I ever did get past the first chapter or not. Next was a string of businesses ranging from collecting worms in the yard to sell for bait, to making bow and arrows, to canoes, to looking for a newspaper route, to building hang gliders. None of them, including the last, ever "got off the ground." I still can't quite put my finger on exactly what it was that put such an entrepreneurial drive into me, perhaps partly being the oldest in the family, or being homeschooled, giving me a personal sense of independence.

The seed of that desire I consider a gift of "grace." It seems to me that those who have that seed know it, it might be small, but it's still there. And some of the tiniest seeds grow into the largest trees. So, for me, the question was how to cultivate that seed, so it becomes a tree of success. The answers eluded me for years, and it seemed life was against me. Everything I tried went sour. One venture to the next, from my late teens into mid-twenties, and all these great ideas (or so I thought!) would stay just out of my grasp. I, among others in my social group, was often heard saying on numerous occasions "a day late and a dollar short" of the opportunities that would seemingly slip through our fingers. "The rich get richer, and the poor get poorer" was our motto, insinuating that we were on the "poor" end of the spectrum.

In the end, I got a job, which was a good thing. I am in full agreement with Robert Kiyosaki in "Rich Dad, Poor Dad," the best reason for having a job is to gain a real-world education. There are lessons to be learned that can be best learned as an employee. First "real" job was as a carpenter building houses. From there, to a sales position at a building materials supplier. After four years, it was time to move on, and being married with two children by this time made it a serious venture, but the desire for something more won out, and we relocated. With the move came the start of yet a new business as an independent building contractor, this time, somewhat successful due to having learned a trade and determination. It wasn't easy, but we got by. Barely.

Fast forward a few years, and that brings us to the recession of 2008, a turning point in the lives of many. Work just dried up to virtually nothing, and it was a tough time in more ways than just financially. During this time, I also met a few key people who were very influential on my thinking, perhaps most importantly in helping me change my view of myself. This combined with the need to do something different to support a family, and the dream of doing more while still alive created a breakthrough for me. It wasn't a huge, radical, change-everything-in-an-instant kind, but a major deciding point that something HAD to change. And the catalyst for bringing that change about for me was FOCUS. Not in the sense of blindly seeing only one thing to the detriment of everything else, but a discipline of mind to not lose sight of the goal. In business, it can be easy to be driven, and forget the other aspects of life. Like being a husband and father, or a friend. So, the focus needs to be on the several aspects of ONE whole. My focus looks like this: Personal development, Relationships, Business. And yes, in that order. I look at this as three sides of ONE triangle.

When discussing focus, usually someone will inevitably mention the fact that you can only ride one horse at a time, a statement I fully agree with, but you do have to take care of multiple aspects of that horse to get anywhere. One must pay attention to what reins you are pulling on, watch for possible obstacles in the path, and stay on the horse all at the same time. You could concentrate only on staying on the horse and successfully do so, but you might get a surprise where you end up! And I think this way of looking at it was the key to unlocking the power of focus for me.

We all know someone who focused very well, but all they focused on was money. Focusing on that single aspect is just like staying on the horse. If that is what they truly wanted, be it far from me to state otherwise, but for most people, I think that gets them somewhere they probably didn't want to go. So as you can see, I have a definite, focused idea of what "focus" means! Though to illustrate what it has done for me, I am going to "focus" on only one side of the triangle- the business.

At the turning point, there was a decision to make. In my field of interest, there was only one way that made sense to move forward with, to make my mark. And that was the quality of craftsmanship. I focused on that product, looking for that particular, yet elusive, level of excellence I wanted. Practically speaking, this was not a pretty sight. It ended up being years of many late nights into the early hours of the morning. Thousands of dollars "wasted" in materials, listening to criticism from experts, and discovering good ideas that weren't. And yet, through it, all progress was made. Not overnight, but slowly my skill improved. I had a coach that made a tremendous difference. He couldn't do what I was doing to save his life but had the ability to help me see myself and my work from another point of view. It was a priceless experience.

Through all this was the key of focus, remaking the decision by the hour if necessary, to not take my eyes off the goal and the vision. I could see what I wanted to create in my mind, and I had to concentrate on it. Not a visualization process that brought magical results, but to not allow that image of who I wanted to be, a master in my field, fade into the background, pressured out by the noise of life. Yes, take care of what needs to be taken care of. If your mother is in the hospital, go and visit her. Maybe even if she's not. But never let the vision fade, DO something every day to bring you closer to your dream. That, to me, is focus. It's living life on purpose. Reminds me of one of Tony Robbin's great quotes,

"One reason so few of us achieve what we truly want is that we never direct our focus, we never concentrate our power. Most people dabble their way through life, never deciding to master anything in particular." - Tony Robbins.

An element of focus that was a challenge for me was to keep it positive. I remember many times, sitting there immediately after making a fatal mistake in a matter of seconds that destroyed hours of careful work. In those moments, the destiny was decided, keeping focused on the vision I wanted to achieve. And even repeating to myself over and over like a mantra, "I can do this, I can do this, I can do this." Then taking several deep breaths before starting over again. It happens by doing whatever it takes to maintain the focus like your life depends on it. Because it does. And this would be especially difficult for those whose close family members and loved ones are NOT supportive of their dream.

And it worked! People began asking for my product. The icons of my field began asking my opinions. I was offered contracts. Something was changing. I had another job to make ends meet by this time in the story. Financially, life was satisfactory. But life can be interesting sometimes, and circumstances came together to help keep me focused, pressure from behind and pull from the front you might say. It was time to make another decision and use what I had learned and move to the next level. Applying the lessons I had learned, and not stopping, has propelled me to the next level. I quit my job and went into business full-time, a daring move for anyone. The focus did not let me down, and today, I am a respected leader in my field, the business is thriving, the future looks bright, and we are just getting started.

The satisfaction of success is immense, and it would be my wish that everyone could experience it. Experiencing success is a life-changing event, once tasted, you can never live without it again.

The beauty of it is that life is a journey and the opportunity to continually experience success is part of that journey, not a goal in the end. True success can actually start the first day a decision is made. I will admit it was hard to feel it then, but looking back, I can see it. I am no different than anyone else; I'm not any more special than anyone else. But the power of a decision, especially the one to live by, a different mindset than before, can separate someone from the rest of the crowd.

I am definitely not done with this success thing, and I think the ultimate success is to help other people to find it. To be the catalyst in someone's life that propels them to the next level. Now, wouldn't THAT be something satisfying to focus on?

Biography

Jason Reid is a self-made entrepreneur who has built several successful businesses. He currently owns and operates Hawkeye Falconry Supply, suppliers of *The Finest Falconry Furniture*, where all products are handcrafted to the highest specifications. He values the skills involved in his specialized field and the unique responsibilities involved in working with birds-of-prey which provides a basis for the qualities needed to be successful in any endeavor.

He has a passion for using these virtues to help others in areas of personal development, finance, and charitable work.

He has been published in American Falconry magazine and was a past columnist for "Feathers and Friends" children's magazine.

His accomplishments include a falcon breeding project that helped with the reintroduction of the once-endangered birds, and he continues to be involved in conservation projects and wild bird rehabilitation efforts.

He is a member of the North American Falconers Association, International Eagle Austringer Association, Indiana Falconers Association, and various other state and regional conservation and educational organizations. He enjoys several outdoor sports including camping and boating, as well as spending time with his family and birds. He currently resides in Fort Wayne Indiana with his wife and four children.

CONTACT INFORMATION

Facebook https://www.facebook.com/JasonReidHawkeye

LinkedIn https://www.linkedin.com/in/jason-reid-a054b7166

Chapter 4
HOW TO WORK LESS, EARN MORE AND LIVE FREE AS A LIFESTYLE ENTREPRENEUR

By Francis Ablola

If you spotted me at Starbucks grabbing my morning double espresso or white mocha, you wouldn't think much.

My normal work attire consists of a t-shirt, basketball shorts and a pair of old flip-flops. Chances are I haven't shaved in a week, and my backwards cap is hiding the fact that I desperately need a haircut.

You'd probably never guess I just wrapped up a marketing campaign for one of my clients that brought in an additional 7-figures in revenue, or that I'm masterminding a project that will bring in thousands of new potential customers in just a few weeks.

I operate under the radar, and that's the way I like it.

I call it being a "Lifestyle Entrepreneur."

I work only when I feel like it, with the people I like investing my time with and do it by my own rules from my Floridian beachfront office overlooking the Atlantic Ocean.

The rest of the time you'll find me at home with my beautiful wife and my bouncing baby girl, traveling the country meeting with fellow "Lifestyle Entrepreneurs," and learning new skills that create massive results for my clients and me.

I love what I do, and it's exactly how I designed it.

I don't say this to brag or boost.

I wasn't born with any special talents or advantages.

I tell you this because it's possible for anyone to design a business that supports YOU and your desired lifestyle.

And if you truly want to earn more, work less and enjoy life, then read this special message below.

I'd like to share with you how I went from a 20-something college dropout to corporate burn out, to living a life of AWESOMENESS by design… and how you can do it, too.

WHY I NEVER WANT TO GROW UP!

It's easy to get lost in what the universe throws at you. Long hours, stressful days, increasing frustration, lost time with family and friends – when you're not in "control of your world," you accept this as status quo.

So many people get caught up in the day-to-day, working for a living and forgetting to create a life.

I know this from personal experience.

Starting out in my professional life, I thought I was doing everything the right way.

I had a good job, at a big Fortune 1000 company, with an impressive title, and an office with a window. Check.

I'm all set, and life couldn't be better, or so I thought.

And all of that's fine if that's what you want. But, if you've got the entrepreneurial bug in your DNA, you'll get antsy quickly.

(My guess is if you're reading this right now, then you know what I mean.)

To me, all the hype about the "grown-up life" was a lie.

You do a good job, work longer and longer hours, sit in more and more meetings, and end up spending more than you make.

I got a plaque and certificate of appreciation.

I wanted more than a plaque, a warm place to sit for eight to nine hours a day, 401K and the cost of living raise every year.

I consider myself fortunate that I found out early in my career that I wanted more, and was willing to go get it.

EARLY WARNING SIGNS

Ever since I was a kid, I've had the "be my own boss" itch. Remember the kid in your neighborhood carrying around a bucket wanting to wash your car, or going door-to-door offering to cut your grass for a few bucks over the summer and on the weekends? Yup, that was me.

And it didn't stop there. At 12 years of age, I had a crew of neighborhood kids going door to door selling our services. We were a growing enterprise. During the week, I hustled selling pixie sticks and bubble gum in the lunch room, a venture not looked upon too kindly by the teachers.

There's a saying that the grade C and D students own businesses, and the A and B students end up working for them.

I'm living proof that this statement is valid. I'm not ashamed to say that I barely made it out of high school and left the university before they could kick me out.

Meanwhile, I was working, learning about business on my own, trying new things, taking risks, taking action and getting results.

Over the years, I've had other ventures... You name it, selling advertising to local shops, web design services, multi-level marketing companies selling everything from gas rebates to groceries online. Some were good; some were bad, some were profitable, some not, but All Learning Experiences.

One of the keys to being an entrepreneur is to be willing to fail forward and do it fast.

I'll admit my first major business attempt after leaving college was a major flop.

I'm thankful for it because I discovered a lot about myself and the people around me, which were both positive.

I was in my early 20's and thought I was unstoppable. I knew it all, and I could do it all.

I had a steady job working for a web development company that I helped build from the ground up, but I got bored and wanted more. (You'll see this is a pattern for entrepreneurs.)

So, I quit with nothing lined up.

To add to the urgency, I had planned in two weeks' time to propose to my high school sweetheart and girlfriend of six years. (She said yes, by the way!)

The next year was filled with uncertainty and total confusion on what I should do next. I filled my days getting my hands on every course, book, and CD and attending every seminar I could to learn how to make my business work.

I took on odd projects; we lived off my new fiancé's first-year teacher salary and racked up thousands on credit cards using advances to pay the rent. I even traded my services for gift certificates to a restaurant.

Yes, I worked for food, literally.

I often tell people the worst thing that can happen if you go out on your own and it doesn't work is you have to get a job.

Well, that's what I did. And because I spent a year developing skills and growing my ability to add value to the marketplace, I made myself more valuable in the workforce which landed me in a prime position using the new skill sets to open career options that a college dropout like me would otherwise not have available.

But by now, you know how I feel about working for someone else. So, as soon as I could, I ventured out on my own again and this time with <u>A New-Found Confidence And Solid Game Plan.</u>

Through my experience, I created a game plan of exactly what I would want my business to look like, and what it would take in time and resources.

My new goal was to create a business that supports my life, and not the other way around. I can, fortunately, say I've thrown out the conventions of traditional business and am operating quietly under the radar and still able to create a fantastic lifestyle for my family.

Here are a few key lessons I've discovered that have allowed me to fulfill my personal and business goals:

<u>Attitude:</u> There's a thin line between success and failure. Winners push beyond past failures; they learn from every experience and use the past to fuel the fire to succeed.

<u>Communication:</u> Your ability to communicate and influence applies in every area of business – working with vendors, team members, clients and, of course, making sales.

Creating a network: Your network equals your net worth. It's often said that your income is a direct result of the five people with whom you spend the most time. I'm a natural introvert, but I've ignored my natural tendencies to build a strong network of top-level players.

Support system: Stop listening to negative people in your life. They won't serve you or help you reach your goals. I've been blessed with a wonderful partner; my wife has been supportive every step of the way. Also, the people I've attracted in my network all share similar goals, and that only serves to push us forward.

Find a mentor: I've been fortunate to have worked with many people who I consider mentors. This is the ultimate shortcut to success – finding someone who has what you want, who's done what you're doing, and who has a proven path to reach your goals.

A business vehicle: What many don't realize is there is so much opportunity just waiting for the armed and ready entrepreneur. You can take your skills and fill a need, or plug into a ready-built system. If the system works, do it.

Risk: Willingness to take calculated risks. Fear stops many people from achieving their goals, but the best way to overcome fear is to face it.

Leverage: Here's the key to freeing yourself from work. Outsource, leverage time and other people's resources. If you don't like doing a repetitive task, don't do it. If you can easily train someone else to take work off your hands, then do it. You'll have more time to work ON your business.

Know your reason why: It's the driver behind everything you do, especially if your goal is to create a lifestyle-driven business.

My *why* is to spend time with my family and enjoy our time together without having to worry about financial restraints. I've been fortunate to be a part of almost every second of my brand-new baby girl's life and watch her grow every day.

This is the lifestyle I've created, by design. And, now that you know it's possible, I hope you will take time to figure out what matters most to you and live your dreams.

Biography

Francis Ablola is a marketing strategist and award-winning business writer. His unique ability to effectively communicate with and influence wide audiences has generated millions in revenue and created tens of thousands of new opportunities for his clients. From Fortune 1000 to garage start-ups, he has been helping companies succeed using highly effective yet unusual advertising.

Chapter 5
YOUR PARTNER IN CRIME: THE SUBCONSCIOUS MIND

By Oliver T. Asaah

What is the subconscious mind? The subconscious is the guardian angel of the conscious mind and the queen motivator of our actions.

The subconscious influences every second of our lives in everything we do or fail to do; it is dictated by programs that have been systematically installed in our subconscious starting from birth. It is our partner in crime that micromanages the roles we play: actors, participants, or spectators in the theatre of life, as the case may be.

Some of these thoughts are empowering while others are disempowering. Disempowering ideas are those that hold us back from exploring, exploiting, and manifesting our passion and unleashing our full potential. Empowering ones help us get closer to our destiny. Many minds focus on disempowering thoughts.

How is the subconscious programmed?

The subconscious is the invisible master pilot of our actions. It *tele*-guides our thinking; our thinking dictates our actions, and our actions show who we are.

What can we do to shape our subconscious to work for us?

In the Nweh and some other cultures in the Cameroons, twins are believed to possess some magical powers: they can bring good and bad luck to their family. Twins can inadvertently hurt family members by inflicting severe pain mysteriously. Upon satisfying their demand, they mysteriously fix their fetish deeds.

Once upon a time, at the age of six, one of my step twin-sisters was upset with me, and she promised to sprain my leg. She kept staring at my right leg. Consequently, after a while when I stood up, I realized I couldn't walk. My right leg was hurting, so I submitted to her magical powers, coaxing her to forgive me and return my leg to normal. Instantaneously, my leg came back to normal.

This belief, like many others, have existed from time immemorial; it is held to be true and inextricably interwoven with the lifestyle of believers. Some beliefs might not be true, but extreme belief and faith make them seem real to us. The subconscious is programmed similarly.

The subconscious is programmed in three ways: persons (family, teachers, mentors, peers, friends, associates), place (environment) and things (experiences, media, books, films). These three dimensions encode the subconscious at varying degrees. They determine who, how, where, when, why we acquire our programs. These questions will facilitate the process of reprogramming our subconscious.

The programming of our subconscious starts from conception. According to Joseph Susedik, "Talking to children in the womb has a tremendous impact on their development." He recommends a calm, serene environment for a pregnant mother. A solemn atmosphere ensures the birth of a child with utter trust in the parent. The Dallas *Times Herald article, May 15, 1982,* wrote that Joseph and Jitsuko Susedik believed any parent can raise brilliant children; they just need phonics, environment, and curiosity; the earlier, the better. (Ziglar 1985).

"Only if the child has complete trust, can he or she be taught. You must teach your children with love, gentleness, and only at a time they are willing to learn," Susedik says.

Also cited by Ziglar 1985, Dr. Carole Taylor, Ph.D., head of the Tolatr Academy in Pittsburgh, Pa., believes once children master phonics, they can read anything, even college texts. Dr. Taylor has daughters, ages 10 and 14, enrolled part-time in pre-med courses in a community college. She applies the person, place and things factors responsible for programming in empowering her daughters.

How can we access programs in the subconscious?

This is a journey into the realm of our being to enjoy human endowments: self-awareness, imagination, conscience and independent will; that differentiates us from animals. Just 'deep' it: (Dig, Employ, Expect, Profit) and the salt and the sweat will yield the malt.

Unlike consulting a doctor when we are sick for diagnostics and prescriptions, we have to DOCTOR ourselves in reprogramming the subconscious; that has been my experience. To me, DOCTOR means: Diagnose, Operate, Cure, Treat, Oxygenate and Respect. The exercise is very personal, serene and engaging.

"Faith is a state of mind which can be induced through repeated affirmations or instructions to the SUBCONSCIOUS MIND through the principle of autosuggestion," said Napoleon Hill.

I started with an insight and ended up with sight; I have seen tangible results in my life such as an impeccable positive mindset, which is the reason I am writing this chapter. My baseline of positive attitude is fantastic, then super fantastic and finally super duper fantastic.

My contagious, positive attitude has given me beatitude at my job site, earning me the nickname FANTASTIC! I have seen colleagues who were less enthusiastic, and other employees who were moody brighten up and raise their level of happiness at least when we meet and communicate. This is the mirror neuron effect as described in positive psychology.

Begin with the outcome in mind. You have to see the project from start to finish by visualizing how the successful result will impact your life. Believe in the magic of believing before the process and see it manifest itself. Take a leap of faith forward into the unknown and see your undertaking bear fruit. If you believe it, it will work for you and vice versa.

Physicians have testified that patients who believe in their prescriptions see the best results.

You can use the following outline to try for yourself:

- Look for a serene place. For instance, take a notepad, flashlight, and pen into a closet.
- Jot down all thoughts that come to mind, both empowering and disempowering.
- Exhaust all thoughts until they begin to repeat themselves.
- Separate programs into group (A) – empowering; group (B) - disempowering.
- Transcribe into positive heading (A): rich, happy, healthy, lucky, generous, successful, likeable, intelligent, confident, strong proactive, good-humored, smiley, blessed, hardworking, attractive … and negative (B): poor, unhappy, sickly, wicket, bewitch, dishonest, stupid, weak, unlucky, quarrelsome, hated, moody, greedy, unattractive, procrastinating, lazy, self-doubt.

Group B will dumbfound and daze you, but it is a crystal ball if harnessed. It will take you to the crest. It demands tremendous personal effort. When the daze is overwhelming, take a break but do not freak; resume after regaining sanity.

Negative programs also come from errors we committed in the past: unrealized dreams and aspirations, unforgiving and retributive attitude learned from unforgiving and avenging people around us, hatred of self/others, liking/love of self/others. The entire process is an ORDEAL: (Open, Right, Developmental, Enforcement, and Action (for) Life). It is the right action. Just be open and enforce it for your personal development. Eventually, your energy will lead to unstoppable synergy.

"You are the way you are because that's the way you want to be. If you wanted to be any different, you would be in the process of changing." said Fred Smith.

We are 100% in control of the process of decoding/re-encoding our subconscious and unleashing potential, just like we are in control of our attitude. The difference is that our negative programs might be influencing our attitude. Let's program our subconscious to work for us.

"The greatest discovery of my generation is that a human being can alter his life by altering his attitude." Said William James.

How can we reprogram the subconscious?

To be blind is bad, but worse is to have eyes and not see." said Helen Keller.

Synchronize the final process; fill the vacuum left by decoded negative programs with positive ones. It is the most difficult but groovy part of the process. Our burning desire to succeed will hone our power to alter the status quo, release our potential and unshackle us.

Unlike our minds, the subconscious works round the clock over our lifetime.

I came up with this formula to clear my path: Steadfast; Proactive; Assertive; Discipline and

Emphatic (SPADE). I decided to pick up my SPADE and dig my goldmine. This metaphor propelled me to un-clutter my mind and get rid of the noise that held me back from moving forward. I apply SPADE in my daily activities.

SPADE forms the north arc; Action forms the south arc, meeting in the middle to form the circle of life. Diameter states: do it now; there is no tomorrow.

The Decoding and Reprogramming Process detailed here is systematic and has worked well for me:

- Understand the original cause of negative programs.
- What fuels programs?
- Negative programs are decoding support systems. (Is it the person, place, or thing?)
- Positive programs: supportive energy. (Is it the person, place or thing?)
- Use answers to handle corresponding situations promptly and assuredly.

- Note positive programs against negative ones.
- Example: rich > poor.
- Replace disempowering programs with corresponding empowering ones.
- Declare, affirm, meditate.
- Celebrate success and progress.
- Repeat process until corresponding positive programs replace negative ones.

I used the mirror technique created by Dr. Laura De Giorgio, a clinical hypnotherapist, in the decoding and encoding procedure. I look at myself squarely in the eyes in the mirror, build trust and bond with myself first. I encourage you to use this technique as well. Look in the mirror, ask self: am I poised for change? And be honest. The mirror reflects our image back to us, facilitates introspection, reaching into the subconscious to install our new software respecting our probing inquisitorial response/drive.

The mirror technique also helps translate our daily mantras, pep ourselves and prime our limitless possibilities. We have to Be, Do & Have respectively. Never try to Have, Be and then Do. Are we taking full advantage of our positive programs? Release their full potential. In the ORDEAL we will face obstacles, objections, mesmerisms, dilemmas... but our faith alone will resuscitate us.

I experienced a rollercoaster in some programs, and momentary crest falls in some. SPADE, daily meditations, declarations, and affirmations helped me get over most of them. Listen and watch motivational and inspirational tapes. Adjust or quit the relational illness environment that is holding you back and develop a nourishing mindset. READ (Rise Every day Above Death) & STUDY (Seek TuneUp Drive Yourself) consistently. Reading is the first step. Studying what you just read tunes you up, so you can apply yourself correctly through acquired knowledge; that is power!

You must take a conscious, meticulous approach to master your new positive programs through practice and exercise and unlearn the negative ones. The more engraved disempowering software was in your subconscious, the harder you have to work to reprogram it. For me, I revisited the reprogramming process several times, and I still do for the hard ones. I believe that the earlier in life one gets this awareness and uses this technique; the more reversible the situation. Once positive ones take root, you must practice and accentuate their benefits to prevent negative programs from resurfacing. The procedure is simple but not easy. Everyone can learn the art, apply the tact, earn the act, tell the facts and sell their story.

My first name is OLIVER (Open Life Invitation Earn Riches). I am inviting you to open up your life by giving reprogramming a chance because I am living proof that it works; this is not pontification. While in the process, I realized that I needed help, an accountability partner. Incidentally, my last name is ASAAH (Asking Seasoned Assistance Always Helps). That's how I decided to make my names acronyms and then put them in full to empower me in all my ventures.

We always need help from a loved supportive one who can hold us accountable and measure our progress, and reprimand us accordingly. It must be someone we trust and respect enough to bestow our life's purpose.

"Were it not for Tenzing the native guide, Edmund Hilary would not have made the historic climb of Mt. Everest." (John Maxwell 1984).

Do not frustrate yourself by expecting exquisite performance initially. Donald Trump's Apprentice became the number one reality show on NBC after several failures, but he chose to follow his instincts and not expert advice; hone your partner in crime for invincible results.

Everyone has empowering and disempowering programs. Just make sure the ratio greatly favors positive programs.

The reality is that 97 percent of the population works for three percent because our programming influences our choices. We can alter that equation by reprogramming our subconscious mind.

Biography

Being one of 24 siblings and having a Bachelor's in Law, Oliver Asaah has a powerful mélange of human relationships. He has several years of experience in network marketing in multiple companies. Oliver is a wellness entrepreneur building one of the biggest organizations in Genewize, a DNA customizing health, wellness & skincare solutions company. He is a speaker and mentor/coach who has a passion for motivating and inspiring people. Oliver has vested and harnessed the power of the subconscious through reprogramming and using his SPADE formula to maximize intuitive energy and synergy for personal and organizational achievement.

Contact Information

Oliver T. Asaah
Wealth Pool Industries
P O Box 1261
Greenbelt MD 20768

Phone: 301 537 2068

oliverasaah@yahoo.com

Chapter 6
THE JOURNEY OF SUCCESS

By Dr. Steven & Dr. Terresa Balestracci

Success is like a recipe; there are many ingredients. So, if there were a recipe for success, what would it be?

Well, perhaps the first step would be to have a dream, a reason, a why. Without this, it would be like going on a vacation without knowing where you are going.

Next, you need to have a plan or a vision. It would be the procedures to get to your destination. Some call it your roadmap.

After that, you would need the desire and passion to get you to your destination. We agree this would be your "fuel" to get you from point A to point B. This is vital to driving you toward your goal.

Next, you need a support team or an accountability partner. This is very important so that you have people to encourage you along the way. This will assist you in overcoming the challenges that you will undoubtedly face.

You may not always have control over some of the challenges that you will face along your journey, but two things you can control are your thoughts and with whom you surround yourself. Achieving success is not easy, but surrounding yourself with people who believe in you, and support and encourage you will accelerate the speed at which you can reach success. This would also include reading books that inspire you to succeed and grow as a person.

Finally, the last step would be to celebrate! When you achieve your goals and dreams and every win along the way, you should rejoice and be thankful for the many blessings that you have.

We believe that a key ingredient to achieving success at any level is having faith, not only in ourselves but most of all, having faith in God. We believe that God puts dreams in our minds and hope in our hearts for a reason. He truly wants us to have the many blessings that he has to offer. We are truly thankful for the dreams and desires that the Lord has placed in our hearts and minds, and the daily courage He graces us with to live them out.

Placed in my heart and the daily courage He graces me with to live them out!

Our favorite quote on success is by George Sheehan which states, "Success means having the courage, the determination and the will to become the person you believe you were meant to be."

We love this quote because it is also the true meaning of success. Nowhere in the quote does it talk about how much money you make or how many material objects you possess. This quote can truly be applied to any person and any situation.

Without courage, you allow fear to prevent you from taking the next step that is vital to achieving success. Without determination, you allow challenges to prevent you from continuing on your path to achieving success.

One of the major challenges that we believe holds people back from achieving success is fear. Overcoming fear is one the most difficult things to do, but if a person does not overcome a fear that is a roadblock to achieving their goals, they will never achieve success associated with that goal or dream.

We believe that any super-successful person has had to overcome many fears and obstacles on their journey to success. And, by pushing through, you will grow as a person and be another step closer to achieving success.

An analogy that we can apply is that of a small child who is trying to walk. First, the child has to have the courage to take the first step and even after they try and try and fall many times, which represents the challenges, they must keep going, or they will never succeed in walking. If this child were to allow their fear of falling to get in the way, they would never even try again.

This is why we believe that it is an innate instinct for us to want to achieve. It is up to us whether we are going to allow the challenges that we face on our journey of success to strengthen us or weaken us. This is simply a decision that we must make that will allow us to turn our challenges into strengths.

To us, success is pursuing your dreams and goals despite the challenges that may occur during the process. We have had many challenges in our businesses and personal lives.

Whether it is a two-month delay in the build-out of our office space, an employee that has stolen from us, one of our kids getting sick, or losing a loved one, we have faced these challenges and never lost sight of our dreams and goals. What we have realized as we have grown over the years through our experiences and education is that the challenges never stop coming, but how we react to them has changed. For example, a situation that five years ago would have distracted us and taken us off the path to our goals for weeks or months, now only lasts for hours or days.

A mindset that we have learned to draw upon is to improvise, adapt and overcome which has allowed us to open our minds and understand that our minds are extremely powerful, so powerful that it brings to mind other quotes we continue to draw upon and try to impress upon others to do the same.

Just a few of these are:

"Whatever the mind can conceive, it can achieve!" and as Henry Ford has said "Whether you think you can or you think you can't…You're right." Something that Yoda said in the Star Wars series, "There is no try, there is only do or not do." Lastly, an important concept that we teach our kids, "Never let anyone's opinion of you become your reality unless it is a Positive opinion!"

We believe the greatest tip we have learned in life and business is forgiveness and being able to leave the past in the past. Not only is it vital to forgive others when they have wronged you, but it is just as important, to forgive yourself.

Not forgiving yourself can destroy your self-worth. And, it can send you down a path of self-destruction and mediocrity. It has happened to us many times in our lives where we were presented with challenges, things that hurt us financially and emotionally, and we dwelled on them and allowed them to steal happiness from our lives and enthusiasm from our spirits.

We have personally seen people in our personal and professional lives who carry baggage from the past and allow it to destroy their lives. They wind up getting ill, mentally and physically and prevent any chance of happiness and success they ever had.

Because of the personal growth and development training that we have experienced, we realized how much they held us back, and delayed and distracted us from our goals and dreams in the pursuit of our success.

We believe that some of the most important keys to achieving success are having desire and passion. We both grew up in Italian-American households where there was a great deal of influence from family members.

Food was always present no matter what the occasion or lack of occasion. The main thing about this combination of family, food, and conversation was passion and desire. These people were very passionate and expressive, to say the least, about what seemed like everything they spoke of, regardless of whether it was a sporting event, last night's dinner or a day at "work."

The majority of them desired to be more successful than the last generation, as was the last generation's desire for them. This love of life and people was a driving force in their pursuit of happiness and success, and has influenced us and helped to define who we are today.

Other major influences that have impacted our lives are our role models and mentors. While we learned from many authors, speakers, and educators, we do have a few favorites.

Two of our favorite role models are B.J. Palmer, developer of chiropractic and world-renowned educator and entrepreneur, and Warren Buffet, world-renowned entrepreneur, and business mogul. They represent success achieved through passion, desire, and vision.

Two of our favorite mentors are Marc Accetta, world-renowned trainer, speaker, and entrepreneur, and Matt Morris, world-renowned best-selling author, speaker, and entrepreneur. Marc and Matt are both incredibly successful people who have taught us so much about life and helped us achieve our current level of success through their guidance, incredible leadership and training. They are passionate about teaching people to achieve the success that they have, which is a quality that we greatly admire.

The thing that we are most passionate about is helping people. This is why we pursued our careers in chiropractic. We feel that chiropractic can positively impact people's lives more profoundly since we, as doctors/teachers, empower people to take a more active role in their health and well-being rather than being victims and passively existing through the symptom-based system that the current healthcare model offers.

We also have passion and desire to help people through our other business in the industry of network marketing and travel. It is with this business that we have learned personal growth and development skills, as well as the skills to create additional streams of income and be able to assist others to achieve the same. As we experience wins in our businesses by helping people, we achieve spiritual and emotional wins for ourselves. This is the satisfaction that continues to motivate us to keep going in our pursuit of success.

Another desire we have as we continue to pursue our dreams is that we make our children proud of us. We believe that the best way we can do this is to live with passion, have the courage to finish what we start and lead by example.

We try to be as mindful of this as possible as we raise our three children. We want them to have their own dreams, and we do not want to live vicariously through them and prevent them from reaching their full potential. Also, we remind them that even when they have a class or subject that they do not have much interest in that they should put forth the effort, because they might just be surprised at the outcome, especially about the growth of self-confidence and self-worth.

When we were growing up, we always had the desire for our parents to be proud of us; however, now that we have kids, they are who we most want to make proud. We feel that achieving this would be one of the greatest successes in our lives.

As parents and successful business owners, we believe that you have to lead by example. Whether you see yourself as a leader or not, many of us are viewed that way because of the actions that we take and the way that we inspire the people around us. Leadership is a combination of many qualities that an individual must possess.

A true leader is someone who can motivate people to take action through communication and representation as well as having the ability to overcome resistance to challenges to attain a common goal for the betterment of both the individual and the team. A great leader, Zig Ziglar, once said, "If you help enough other people get what they want, you get what you want."

Finally, for us, we have realized that success in a culmination of many components with some of the main ones being faith, vision, passion, desire, belief, courage, resilience, attitude, humbleness, integrity, honor, purpose, leadership, knowledge and the application of knowledge.

We are truly blessed and humbled to have the opportunity to share some of our thoughts on success to positively impact the lives of others with the hopes that this will assist them on their journey of success.

Biography

Dr. Steven & Dr. Terresa Balestracci met in Davenport, Iowa, while attending Palmer College of Chiropractic where they both graduated with Doctor of Chiropractic degrees. They have owned a successful chiropractic office in Bridgewater, New Jersey, for over 15 years. They have been involved in network marketing with a company called WorldVentures where they rank in the top 1% of the company's independent representatives. Michael, Gianna, and Cristian, their three children, inspire them to strive to achieve higher levels of success and for whom they desire to leave a legacy.

Contact Information

Dr. Steven & Dr. Terresa Balestracci
Phone: 484-375-5380 / 484-375-5385
Address: 2385 Silvano Dr., Macungie, PA 18062

Chapter 7
25 Birthday Cakes

By Blake Fleischacker

As I sit here and type, I realize that I have lived a longer life than some, but a shorter life than most. Ornaments have hung from 25 Christmas trees. Candles have flickered on top of 25 birthday cakes. I can say that I have lived one-quarter of a century and I have spent it looking up.

I think that is the byproduct of being the youngest of three children, as well as being raised by eternal optimists. Negativity was not allowed in the house, even if he took his shoes off at the door.

Aside from hiding vegetables under the placemat and in the dog's mouth, my dinners were spent listening to Dad's sermons on the value of manual labor and manners while mom programmed us to be thankful for one thing every day. I am fascinated by how much I have grown to appreciate the fundamentals that were discussed at the dinner table.

Birthday Cakes 0-14

My Velcro shoes walked me to elementary school until I learned the power of shoelaces. My Ninja Turtles backpack usually contained a few items of homework and a packed lunch. For a while, I was cute.

My freckles drew in the ladies while I was a young boy, but they soon faded into the most severe case of acne the local dermatologist had ever seen. Entering the teens with a research-worthy dose of acne taught me the cold reality of having a visible stigma. Classmates came to know me for my face rather than my friendship.

Heavy medications were taking a toll on my body. Weekly facial injections were taking a toll on my spirit. Little did I know that success insights were at the end of the fingers that pointed out my damaged skin.

In a technology-based world where we can work from home and type to talk, it becomes difficult to walk a mile in someone else's shoes. I was grateful when people would try seeing life through my eyes. It reminded me that I was welcome, I was human, and I was still entitled to student success. As a result, I now surround myself with people who work hard to account for the other side of every story.

If people are cut off on the highway, the majority grow angry and make it known. There are a select few who remind themselves that there may be good intentions behind that person's actions and important details that are missing in the scenario. Someone may be rushing to their wife who is going into labor.

Someone may be running out of time to visit their dying child. Success means taking the time to exercise empathy. In doing so, you will learn more about yourself and others.

Birthday Cakes 15-18 (Summer)

My white dress shirt, snoopy tie and black apron was the uniform that customers saw as I stood behind the checkout packing groceries. My first summer job was as a grocery clerk at the local store by my cottage.

My reference points for success were a fully loaded section of soda, a long row of shopping carts and a bag packed with the eggs and bread on top.

Looking back, I did not even realize the true value I was bringing to the customers. I knew that the cans needed to be stocked with the labels facing out. I knew that the carts were to be collected every 30 minutes.

I did not appreciate the big picture back then, but I do now. I worry that many of us fail to appreciate the greater power of the work people do in this life. Grocery clerks do not stock shelves; they feed families.

911 telephone operators do not receive calls; they save lives.

Taxi drivers do not just drive; they enable people to perform their daily lives. I define successful people as those who go out of their way to remind individuals of their true significance in this world. Let people know what would not be possible without them. Go out of your way to deliver a thoughtful, meaningful thank you for the work that people do.

Birthday Cakes 15-18

My hand clenched the handle on my trumpet case as I entered the doors of high school. School band was one of my passions during my life between the lockers. Without passion, it is practically impossible to achieve success.

My involvement in the arts earned me more ridicule than respect. Excited to make music, I accepted the ridicule and trusted that respect was around the corner. I was right. Deciding to pursue my passions granted me entrance into greater circles of opportunity. I dove into student leadership and was able to be on a team that impacted the success of the entire school community.

I connected with teachers and learned their secrets to success.

Eventually, people realized my commitment and decision to be comfortable in my own skin.

"You can never make the right decision. You can only make decisions, and then make them right." I heard that quote from my dad, and he likely heard it from someone else. Regardless of its source, the quote is my favorite mantra.

It helped with the daily decisions of high school and all the decisions that followed. Success is built on a series of wise decisions, and I am overjoyed that I decided to follow passion rather than punks.

Music was my way of showing my personality, and my personality helped me deliver the speech as the student-elected Valedictorian. By the end of high school, I had learned the power of always showing your personality because you never know who may be watching.

Birthday Cakes 18-25

My Buzz Lightyear bedsheets were a definite conversation piece in my university residence room. *I could list the common lessons that people can lift from their post-secondary textbooks, but my foundations for life and leadership were laid in residence.*

My student and then professional life in residence combined for a total of seven years and 6,000 roommates.

I was passionate about the community spirit in residence, so I decided to stay involved. As soon as I graduated, I was hired to be a Residence Manager. In a world that becomes even more of a melting pot, I can say that I was privileged to learn what life is like being a neighbor to a collection of cultures.

Developing relationships made university fun, but developing community made university meaningful. Students moved in at the start of each year as strangers, and I had the opportunity to help them connect with family. I was a member of a team of people that worked to serve the needs of young adults.

We saw the good, and we saw the bad. We saw the happy, and we saw the sad. Success was found in the student who overcame homesickness. Success was found in the roommate relationship that was getting repaired. Success was found when a student considered giving up on life, and we connected them to resources to get back on track. Residence life exposed me to the intricacies of human life. I grew to understand that humans share more similarities than differences. We all have a story, and it is developed in that space between our arrival and our exit on this earth. I learned that successful relationships require hard work and successful communities require even harder work.

All the Other Birthday Cakes

As a 25-year old, I have spent more of my life at my parents' dinner table than on my own.

The dinner conversations sent me successfully through my first 25 years of life. As eternal optimists, mom and dad's commitment to the bright side enabled me to draw the value of empathy out of the struggle of acne.

The routine, manual labor is what taught me the value of hard work and the bigger picture behind stocking shelves and collecting carts. Eliminating negativity is why I was drawn to the positive experiences derived from my passions in high school.

Saying thank you is what kept me invested in residence life. Leaving home, I decided to make my parents proud and thank everyone who made a positive impact on me during university. When you appreciate the world around you, opportunities begin to present themselves. That is why I stayed. My parents are my role models for success. The most important thing I learned about success is from them: Say thank you to the people who have made you successful along the way.

Bob and Judy Fleischacker, consider this my thank you. You have helped me lay the foundation for my next 25 years, and I guarantee that I will commit it to paper. Perhaps I will begin next week when I blow out the candles on my 26th birthday cake.

BIOGRAPHY

Blake Fleischacker lived and worked with over 6,000 students during his profession as a Residence Manager at The University of Western Ontario. As the author of "Campus Gets Wasted" and having spoken to over 10,000 students and professionals, Blake is a highly sought after trainer and keynote speaker. Blake is blessed to have an outstanding family and girlfriend who inspire him to write.

CONTACT INFORMATION

Blake Fleischacker
1-877-987-4359

Chapter 8
ESSENTIAL SUCCESS: "A LIVING RANSFORMATION"

By Ray Blanchard, Ph.D.

If you knew you only had a short time to live, and then it's going to be over, what would you do with the rest of your life?

This message is for individuals who desire to succeed beyond measure and who are urgent to live their true potential. That means living with purpose and passion. That means having the courage to dream big and to go after what you want like the present is all you have. In this crash course on self-transformation, several basic understandings and distinctions are shared so you can flip the switch to your success. It will be the reader's challenge to live such wisdom and to keep those distinctions alive.

My story may be like yours, a typical "zero to hero" scenario. It reveals lessons for a clear path to change lives for the better. It is amazing how these humble beginnings built such a solid foundation for the achievements that followed.

I am one of 12 children, born to a strong-willed Mississippi farmer. I am the youngest of six sons. My mother always stressed learning from your hardships and moving on without complaining and giving something to your neighbors along the way. Life was a struggle for my parents, always barely making ends meet. Finally, when I was about 12 years old, the ravages of a tornado tearing through the little shotgun house we lived in forced us to pick up and leave the farm my father worked since he was born some 66 years earlier. I had been a "smart" little kid in the country school where my aunt was the principal, and most of the grades were in the same room.

But, moving to the big city in St. Louis, I was quite unprepared to compete with my classmates initially. Not liking that, I worked hard to prove myself, to help the family out and make my parents proud. I got a job in a grocery store and ran a newspaper route. I paid for my clothes and school supplies. By the second year in high school, I was able to start sports, where I learned to strive even harder and always aim to win. By taking a new job in the morning before school at the local hospital and running two miles through the park to make it to morning classes, I became a good athlete and student. My counselors took notice of my efforts and decided to help me get into college since my parents would not have been able to help me at all. Forging ahead with encouragement from my advisor, I finally got a break. I went to night school at Washington University in St. Louis until I earned the opportunity to go full time. One professor took a special interest in me, after noticing my love for classical philosophy, and helped me to get two degrees and a fellowship to a doctoral program where I excelled.

Two key mentors pushed and goaded me to keep moving until I graduated to become a Doctor of Philosophy in Psychology after a little more than three years. My proudest moment was when my mom was able to come 2,000 miles on her first airplane flight to see the first of her brood get an advanced college degree. Since then, other mentors at significant stages of my life helped me go to the next level of success, through the wisdom they had gained and imparted to me. The unbelievable support from these life coaches has taken me around the world in more ways than one and has stewarded me to extraordinary accomplishments and joy. I feel blessed and grateful, and I live with the passion for giving back.

The greatest success lesson in all my experiences is to *"always believe,"* especially when the light is dim, and there doesn't seem to be a way out. Keep your belief strong and determined to outlast the challenges. Don't ever give up on what matters. You often gain the victory in the darkest hour, by that one extra heave or burst of effort like your life depended on it. In the race for life, it's that last act that gives you victory or marks the final arrival of a long journey.

The completion of a heartfelt commitment is the ultimate arrival. But, it is the process of getting there with joy and passion that is the best and most meaningful. If you can live your life with joy and ease while attaining satisfaction in personal, professional and spiritual affairs, you are a success.

On your way to the top, it is important to give back and help someone else. *"Reach back and pull someone else up."* Pay it forward. This is both satisfaction for you, and it makes a difference in the social consciousness of the world. These are the yin and yang of a principled life, and the most important character traits in achieving complete success – getting results and being a giver.

Four key factors are always present in my successes and are most often in those giants we revere as well: (1) hard work, (2) knowledge, (3) attitude and (4) love of God or the Almighty.

Hard Work

Let's face it - life can be tough. Not many successes have been authentically achieved without hard work. That does not mean that life has to be hard. It just means be prepared and go the extra mile. Make it a practice.

For instance, if you are exercising, do a few more minutes or add a few extra repetitions. It is well established that the greatest consistent results come from the extra efforts rather than the easy actions with which you start.

In relationships, you should stretch yourself and have a few more authentic conversations with loved ones and colleagues each week. You will quickly realize that you have super-powered your network of support. Support is vital to being the best you can be and to giving peak performances. Plus, you tend to open up a lot more opportunities and possibilities, personally and professionally, because you reached out.

Refrain from having to be "right" in every conversation. "Being Right" is a social disease and an addiction that destroys relationships on all levels. At least two or three times a week, be conscious of your impulse to dig in your heels to argue your point. Then "let it go." Create win-win interactions and experiences that will uplift your friendships and open more space for everyone to grow. All will be happier and healthier for it, and it is widely believed to add a few more years to your life as well.

These acts may take more focused awareness of your relationships, but the rewards are worth it in terms of your experience of success. You shape the consciousness landscape that surrounds you and enhance your social capital among your peers.

Also, invest a few hours a week in personal growth and inner development activities. The value you gain accumulates and even compounds. By the end of a month, you will notice a big difference. By the end of a year, you will have put in almost a week's investment into yourself. Remember that, after your maker, YOU are the ANSWER and the key to your success.

I strongly suggest pursuing effective empowerment seminars as well. You can learn more about yourself sometimes from such outside sources than you can ever learn from your already existing views of life. I had a true "enlightenment experience" in a seminar in the early years of my professional life, which was life-altering. I treasure it to this day. It could be like that for you, too.

KNOWLEDGE

Knowledge is the key to power. And, power is the ability to turn possibility into reality. The first principle of knowledge is to "know thyself." To accomplish that, one needs to examine his life and see what makes himself tick thoroughly. Sorting through your past experiences and beliefs can tell you why you feel, think and do what you do, and why you get the results you get. Realizing this gives you access to your life script and behavior patterns at the root level, thereby allowing you to create a new map or blueprint for success.

You should practice going into deep thought a few minutes a day to specifically examine the genesis of various beliefs you have, and make corrections that would lead to more expertise, free choice and precise actions that create the results you want. Learn to use the "stop-look-listen" process for self-reflection and life improvement. Stop being on auto-pilot and reactive behavior. Look at life from a new angle or perspective. Listen to your heartfelt commitment rather than negative self-talk. This will help you to make strides toward your higher goals steadily.

Also, take time to reflect on the material you read each day, and examine it from different angles and understandings. Don't be a "yes" machine. Challenge ideas. This is a practice in discipline and critical analysis, which enriches your creativity and ability to invent new possibilities.

You should dedicate an extra two hours a week focusing on a hobby. It will keep you fresh and will likely play a part in the rest of your career, by adding richness and a new dimension to whatever you do. The added time per year that you put into your deeper interests and career will put you heads and shoulders above your peers and will give you the competitive edge to increase your chances for greatness.

Attitude

All reality is dictated by the context that supports it. Positive thoughts lead to positive attitude and actions, and negative ones lead to negative outcomes. In effect, thoughts are things. It would be prudent to deliberately train your attitude and thought processes to generate your desire. This is the key to flipping the switch to success.

Several years ago, one of my good friends who had a less-than-pleasant attitude came to this realization and did something about it, and it significantly shifted his business. He made a paradigm shift to accentuate the positive and eliminate the negative. He started a slogan for his company and followed it: *"I shall not complain."*

He made it a point to eliminate at least a few complaints a day, noting each time he interrupted his negative thoughts. The impact of eliminating several hundred negative imprints a year altered his outlook and ultimately created more customers. Consider doing the same exercise for a year. Include thoughts about your job, family, neighbor, the weather, love life, bank account, the economy, friends, etc. *"You reap what you sow."* Change your mind and change your life.

LOVE OF GOD OR THE ALMIGHTY

The human condition is the continuous search for meaning and fulfillment. This usually brings up our spiritual reality, what sustains us and supports our reason for being.

Truth and meaning are a matter of interpretation. We are continuously interpreting and assessing our spiritual reality, making meaning out of it, and using our interpretations and meanings to act in ways we think would fulfill our lives.

Regardless of how one arrives at their conclusion, the majority of well-known great achievers indicate that material success alone is meaningless, and success without having a sense of fulfilling a higher purpose is emptiness.

Some people, for instance, interpret that there is a greater source of life and meaning outside of our own interpretation, and it is our pleasure to serve It. Some do not. We get to choose for ourselves, which is true for us. Our happiness and motivation often depend on it. For me, the Almighty source of life and meaning is God.

The pursuit of meaning or truth is a very personal and private matter. The sooner you begin the quest, it is to your advantage. Regardless of what you discover, the act of giving and making a difference through service seems to be on the right path to finding out. It provides the most empowering sense of purpose and deep satisfaction that propels us to achieve.

Contributing to world transformation and peace are popular undertakings. Healing the environment, ending hunger on the planet or providing health needs to the sick are also possibilities. Serving your community, church or charity are other ways to quell the thirst. Contributing a few hours of service a week will culminate in several weeks a year of giving to others and making a difference. It makes you feel good about yourself. It is life-redeeming, and it powerfully affects your sense of value.

Success is determined by how well you live your life. Wealth, character or a combination thereof, are the measures. The defining factors include: the risks you take, the courage you demonstrate, the ease in letting go of disappointment and pain, the ability to shift your points of view and come off "autopilot," the ability to think and create possibility in the face of the impossible, how you include people and bring them forward, the patience and love expressed and received, and the difference you make in the lives of others.

Leaders possess these qualities in abundance, and in sharing them, they make the difference between potential and reality. *"Having what it takes and not using it is a waste, but living such qualities can transform the world."*

Success is self-realization. Being real and being oneself is the most one can be. Our challenge is to strive for such completeness so that we reach the pinnacle of human achievement and excellence. My favorite quote, *"To thine own self, be true,"* captures it succinctly.

The way of the Buddha is an exquisite example. It is the way of ease, where effort and effortlessness are balanced in perfect harmony. It demonstrates integrity, which is *Essential Success.* The life of Jesus is a perfect model of success in action, handling challenges and relating to others. He is an example of acceptance and inclusion, never giving up, purpose and passion, and overcoming while still loving - *A Living Transformation.* Together they represent our ultimate goal, which is to be whole, perfect and complete. And that is *Essential Success: A Living Transformation.*

Biography

Dr. Ray Blanchard, the founder of Blanchard Consulting Group, is a seasoned entrepreneur, consultant, and media producer. He earned his Ph.D. from the University of Oregon and garnered praise for his films *THE ANSWER To Absolutely Everything* and the *FIRESIDE FORUM*. With more than 100,000 client-graduates worldwide, he was elected to the esteemed *Transformational Leadership Council*.

Contact Information

Dr. Ray Blanchard
youcountnow@gmail.com
541-912-8571
www.rayblanchard.com

CHAPTER 9
JOURNEY TO "SUCCESS"

By Crystal Wolfchild

I am a Dakota woman. I was born December 20, 1981, at home in Burbank, Calif., surrounded by crystals, in the hue of blue light. I emerged as Crystal Dawn Wolfchild. I was fortunate to grow up nurtured by loving parents who raised me in the balance between the modern and traditional worlds.

My connection to the "Creator" and "Mother Earth" grounded and supported me from the beginning. My first Sweat Lodge Ceremony was at eight weeks, and Sundance Ceremonies blessed my summer months. At four years old, I was given my spirit name, Morningstar Woman. The teachings of my ancestors, the "Star Nation," guided my life. With my strong foundation, I knew that success was at hand. Little did I know that success had many different faces.

It wasn't until my father told me the stories of my people that the harsh realities set in. We were on a road trip one summer, passing through Mankato, where dad told me of the 38 Mdewakanton Dakota men who were executed in 1862. This was the largest mass execution in the history of the United States, and nobody seemed to know it!! The stockade was built specifically to drop all 38 men at the same time, and when it came time on Dec. 21, the original hanging date, they didn't have enough rope to hang all of them at once. So, President Abraham Lincoln rescheduled for the day after Christmas. On that day the town's people, families, women, and children, came to witness the gruesome event. My whole world was struck; pain coursed through my body and hot tears flooded my soul. I was in disbelief. How could this happen and why?

If that wasn't bad enough, Lincoln ordered to kidnap and hang two more men a year later; one of the men was my grandfather, Medicine Bottle.

I didn't know what was more disturbing, that this travesty had taken place, or that it was never talked about, taught in schools or acknowledged! I was outraged. My mind was racing; my body was aching, and millions of questions flooded my world. How can we praise Lincoln who freed the slaves, but fails to mention that he also ordered the hanging of 38 men the day after Christmas in 1862? This was but one of many historical events that failed to be recognized, much less healed.

This knowledge was a huge part of my awakening. I realized the historical trauma and a 'deep depression' within the psyche of native people. I recognized the mental constructs and the depth of this wounded paradigm, from which my people were acting and resulting in alcoholism, high rates of suicide and health problems, etc. Though I was not a statistic, I was heartbroken. I was seeing what was happening to my people, heritage, culture, and traditions.

We were getting lost in the story of what had happened. I saw the story as a lie, and that peace lay within every one of us. This was a powerful breakthrough for me.

My heart yearned for the truth which brought me to the next leg of my journey: healing, forgiveness, and wholeness. 2004 marked the beginning of a memorial horse ride honoring the 38 plus two men that were hung in Mankato. Jim Miller, a Dakota man, had a dream; some people would call it fruition, calling or vision. Around the same time, I heard my calling. Our ancestors and the universe were speaking, lighting a path to freedom.

On the memorial of the hanging, Jim rode on horseback with many riders to Mankato. For four days, they rode for reconciliation and forgiveness, healing the past and honoring the men and families whose lives were deeply impacted in order to heal those lives still being affected today. The horse ride was a huge success! It brought the people together in a common goal, to heal and honor the past. To be in Dakota is to walk in peace with all living things. We were coming home to what is true.

My vision mirrored that of the horse ride and Jim's dream. My healing of personal hurts and trauma came through the Sundance ceremony and Transformational work. Everything was leading me back to the spirit and my truth. What I learned through the transformational work was that to heal I had to accept what is, harvest the lesson or gift that was birthed out of the event, and release and let go of the past, moving forward like the buffalo. I could stand in the truth of what is now, the present, and what has always been. The beauty and power of what it is, to be Dakota, to be alive, to be a human being in this magnificent world!

The so-called history were events that happened at a time in a place. I realized I was the creator of the meaning of that event and from which certain belief systems were born. The freedom came from knowing that the events happened, but that it did not define me, or take anything away from me as a native woman. I realized I had a choice! I could choose to be a victim and let something in my past take over my life, make me angry, sad, depressed, or I could choose peace and live my truth and divine right, to be joyful, free and prosperous. I know who I am today, and I honor the history and past events because I choose to see the beauty and gifts within. I get to be the change I want to see... to walk in peace with all living things... to stand in my principles of unconditional love, unity, peace, and joy!

Today as I write, I am much more than a Dakota woman - a spiritual being, an artist, a lover, a friend, teacher, student, a powerful, courageous, passionate, loving woman. I choose at any moment who I am and what I want to create, through me, in me, as me... BEING whatever I declare. I choose a life of unlimited possibilities from which anything can be accomplished.

In my life, I do many things, and although they are all significant, they do not define me or make me who I am. One of my passions is the art of make-up application. I remember as a child growing up playing in my mom's makeup; I was the four-year-old Picasso! I was brilliant, I tell you!! Ok, maybe not brilliant in technique at age four, but that fire fueled my passion for working on the live canvas and brought me to a successful career in makeup.

My credits and acknowledgments could prove my "success," but no award nor credit proved my success to me. It was the embodiment of love, joy, and gratitude that showed me what success really is.

Success is doing what you love. It can be BIG or small, neither one more significant, but equal as long as you are living your truth. Never settle for mediocrity if that is the way the cookie is crumbling, so to speak; check within! You might be pretending not to know something and be doing what you think is the "right" thing. After all, there is no "wrong" or "right." Your results will speak for themselves! They say that if you want to know your intention, take a look at your results! If you don't like something, do something different! Whatever you do, do it 100 percent, wholeheartedly. Do what inspires you and ignites your soul! Trust and listen to your body; it will never lie to you. Follow your bliss; your heart will lead you! Let your spirit be your guide, and all the abundance and prosperity will follow as a result of following your true nature.

Today, I choose to be an artist, authentic and true to creating art on a live canvas. I work on people of every shape, color, and size, each uniquely beautiful and perfect.

I found adventure in the entertainment world and began my makeup journey at the age of 19, fresh out of high school.

In the past 10 years, I've been fortunate to have worked on TV and film such as "American Idol," "Nip/Tuck," "Heroes," "America's Got Talent," "So You Think You Can Dance," "CNN's Larry King Live," "Superhero Movie," "School For Scoundrels," and many more.

I have been nominated for two EMMY's for "So You Think You Can Dance" and received a First American In the Arts Award for Outstanding Achievement in Technical Arts for Make-Up! I know that because I love what I do I have created these results for myself. I continue to listen to the song of my soul, and it leads me to where I go next. I live in gratitude for my abundantly ever prosperous career and have many visions much bigger for the world.

I am forever grateful to keep expanding and expressing my life's dance... and be a leader in the evolution of the planet through love. Through the history of my people, I realized that life wasn't "perfect," that everyone has a story to tell, hurts, and sadness but also victories and triumphs of overcoming. I realized that no matter the history or the story, human beings are resilient, creative, unique beings. That whatever happened in the past does not define and determine who we are or who we ever were, but standing in the space of who and what I choose to be in this moment. I am and have always been a "success," because I always had love in my heart.

Biography

Crystal Wolfchild: As a Visionary, innovative Make-up Artist, and Spiritual Being, Crystal Wolfchild stands for a world of infinite possibilities. A creative force in the make-up world Crystal is the recipient of a First Americans in the Arts Award for Outstanding Achievement in Technical Arts for Make-Up in 2008 and has been Nominated twice for an Emmy award for her work on "So You Think You Can Dance."

Her unique style and exquisite talent have reached top shows such as "American Idol," "Nip Tuck," "Heroes" and the "Super Hero Movie." She has worked with talents such as Kelly Carlson, David Cooke, Cat Deely, Julian McMann, Chris Brown, Tiffani Thiessen, Hugh Laurie and many more.

Besides living her true passion as an artist, she exemplifies leadership in her community by being in service through Love, Prayer and transformational work. Crystal envisions a world where everyone gets to know and experience themselves as the true gift they are, and that each person makes a difference in their unique expression of themselves on the Planet. One world, one heart, one love is her mission through her business, in which she teaches women all over the country and the world the art of self-expression through makeup application.

CONTACT INFORMATION

Crystal Wolfchild
818-326-0525
wolfchildcrystal@yahoo.com

Chapter 10
Reaching Success with Excellence

By Ellen Reid

It seems like every day I wake up, and there's something new and different about my industry. And I don't mean some little change; I'm talking about something earthshaking, life-changing, revolutionary.

Okay, maybe it's not every day. However, it started a few years ago, and the momentum is most definitely building. I work in the publishing industry, specifically the self-publishing end of it. I've been involved in this exciting field since 1998, and I have seen what feels like a century's worth of changes take place in just over a decade. These include things like digital printing, print on demand, and, most recently, e-books and readers.

However, one thing I have observed to be constant is that those authors and books that have been successful – and in fact, people who are successful in any area of endeavor, whether business or personal life – are those that demonstrate excellence. I have made excellence the cornerstone of my success.

"Excellence" has become my mantra, my branding, and my way of life. I'm not saying that excellence will guarantee success. However, I can't imagine real success without excellence being a part of it.

I wouldn't say excellence has always been a part of my life. However, it is something that was tempered in the fires of my life's adventures. My father was of the narcissistic persuasion, so no matter what I accomplished it somehow became about him. I soon learned that he demanded perfection, which, even to this day, I don't believe is possible. However, I was continually striving to do better and better. I may have missed perfection, but I guarantee you, I developed a real track record of excellence.

As I grew and matured, pursuing studies in personal growth, I came to learn how to transform my feelings of frustration with my father's unattainable demands into positive motivation to excel. Whether it was in my first career in sales and marketing, where I rose up the ranks to international buyer, frequently being sent to Asia to develop products, or my current consulting/book shepherding career, in which I have been acknowledged Beverly Hills' Premier Book Consultant, I found myself compelled to both produce excellence and encourage others to it.

Excellence is an interesting concept. People know it when they see it, but they may not know *why* they recognize something as excellent.

In my work, there are certain definite guidelines for what excellence is not. For example, typos in a book are a sure sign of less than excellent work — and this erodes the value of the message. So, for me, one major element of excellence is attention to detail.

That can be reflected by a well-proofread galley, which is pretty evident to everyone. But, it can also be reflected in subtle things like the amount of space between lines on a page (called leading – which is a term taken for the days of hand-setting type with individual letters cast from metal, like lead, and adding a line of lead in between the lines) or the amount of space between letters, called kerning. (I have no idea why they call it that.)

Another thing – one of those changes I was talking about – is that computers instill a false sense of ability. Anyone with a computer and Microsoft Word can create what may look like an actual book. But it's not, which you can tell when you compare a page done in Word with a page done by a professional with a page layout program. This leads me to another big tip: Know when you can handle something yourself and know when it will serve you to bring in a professional.

When it comes to excellence, professionals are worth their weight in platinum. What I have observed is that some people are great at some aspects of their work, mediocre at other aspects and downright poor at others. So, one key I've found for myself and that I share with clients is to evaluate what's necessary for any task and determine which you can legitimately do yourself and which you need help to do.

I counsel people to be ruthless with themselves and not be afraid to admit there are just some things they're not great at doing. While there may be some subtle message in our culture that says we're supposed to be able to do everything ourselves, in my experience, it's the very rare person who can do it all with excellence.

With writers, the things they need to look at include the actual writing of their book. Even the biggest names in the business, authors who have made millions and published lots of books, will tell you that one of their greatest assets and allies is their editor. While you may not be an author, you most likely do write letters for your business. Make sure they are well proofed, if possible by someone other than you. Catch all the typos, make sure it looks good on the page, neither too high or too low on your letterhead. Make sure your point is stated and what you are asking the recipient to do is specific.

Okay, I know you may not send a lot of letters, but I'll bet you send several emails each day. While some of the ideas above may not apply, do proofread your emails for typos and grammar. And make sure what you're saying is clear.

Back to my writing clients. Not only do they need to start by making sure their manuscript is in excellent shape, but they also need to have a powerful cover. This means they need to get a book cover designer, not the daughter of a friend of theirs who did very well in her college design class. Book design is a specialized field and not every good graphic designer knows the ins & outs of book cover design. Ditto interior design. You would be amazed at the difference in readability when a good interior book designer gets hold of a manuscript.

Presumably, you can translate what I'm saying here to your own life and business. If you are putting something out that represents you or your business – and I mean anything from a wedding invitation to a printed brochure – make sure it's done right, by a professional if necessary, if you want it to reflect excellence. And do your homework; if you're looking for a professional, don't just pick the first name that comes up when you google graphic designer. Part of excellence is following up with samples of work and references from others who have used the person's services.

Another area that comes up for my clients is promotional writing. On books, that's everything from the title and subtitle, to the back cover and the short author's bio. What I often have to communicate with my clients is that just because they can write an excellent book does not mean they can write the text that is needed to sell their masterpiece. Again, it's a matter of finding a professional who can articulate what you're offering in a way that potential customers will recognize it as having value to <u>them</u>. My experience is that many – maybe most – people are so close to their message, product, or service, that they want to tell everyone about all of it. A good promotional copywriter will be able to advise on how much needs to be said to generate interest, and how much is so much information that you lose interest.

Bottom line, what I preach and what I practice is that the right resource people – those who demonstrate excellence – will contribute to my excellence. And that contributes to my success.

Which brings me to the question, what is success?. When I was younger, I thought success was easy to measure. It had to do with how much money you made. Then, after I had made a fair amount of money, I discovered that I didn't feel particularly successful.

So, I began exploring success from the inside out, which involved things like spirituality and personal growth. Those explorations revealed many avenues that I am still considering and dealing with myself. This is a lot like peeling away layers of an onion in that there's always another layer to work through. I expect these pursuits to be ongoing pretty much as long as I've got a body and am here on this earth.

In the end, it was probably this inner questing that brought my awareness to excellence. I find that to have genuine satisfaction in my life, I not only need to have balance in my life but I also need to make sure that I am feeling fulfilled by what I am doing. I am driven to do excellent work and to have my work reflect the excellence of who I am– and, in a very real sense the excellence of who we all are. I find great satisfaction in encouraging my clients to be more of who they can be.

I can't tell you how great it feels to hear how thrilled a client is when they receive their book from the printer and hold it in their hands for the first time. In virtually every case, they tell me that it's far beyond what they had ever envisioned. They feel great, and I feel good because I know they have achieved something they can be very proud of – because it reflects excellence.

Biography

Ellen Reid is a Book Shepherd extraordinaire. Since 1998 she has been assisting authors in exceeding their dreams for an outstanding book they can be proud of, and that stands up to any competition. Acknowledged as Beverly Hills' Premier Book Consultant, Ellen has built her career on excellence. She is the author of the award-winning *Putting Your Best Book Forward; A book shepherd's secrets for creating award-winning books that sell*.

Contact Information

Ellen Reid
Book Shephard
(310) 862-2573
ellen@bookshep.com

Chapter 11
BECOMING THE MAN IN THE ARENA

By Mikel Erdman

I grew up on a farm in southwestern Oregon, in a very small town named Bandon. It's famous now because a rich guy from Chicago came and built some of the top-rated golf courses in the world there. When I was growing up, it was nothing like that. It was a sleepy coastal town surviving on the final feast of the logging and fishing industries and very little else.

My dad was in the meat business just like his father before him, and his grandfather before him. In the summers, we fished our commercial salmon troller for Chinook and Coho salmon and occasionally took off after albacore tuna if they came close enough to the shore. Working these businesses meant long hours and sore muscles and a lot of ingenuity and resourcefulness to stay afloat.

I was surrounded by hard work while growing up, the kind of work that they would feature on the television show "Dirty Jobs." In fact, these were the type of jobs that you had to have a whole different set of clothes for work than you'd ever wear for anything else. It was next to impossible to get the smells out once you've worn them around the feedlot or in the back end of the boat with diesel fumes, fish innards, and cow manure.

From as early as I can remember, I was doing chores and participating in the family businesses. Believe it or not, just growing up in that small business, the do-it-yourself atmosphere had a lot to do with me achieving a high level of success in my life. I learned a whole lot of lessons about dealing with adversity and rising to the challenge.

I saw the magic of new ideas formulated in my mind and then brought to reality by the power of vision, dedication, and persistence. And I learned one of the most important lessons about success right there in the middle of those hard, dirty jobs — that not all good ideas work out and true success comes to those who are willing to face their failures and step out once again to achieve their dreams.

In fact, if you look at some of the most successful people in the world, their careers never shoot to the top without any challenges or setbacks along the way. Some of the most respected and revered leaders in our land seemed to be just a long string of failures accentuated by moments of greatness and characterized by the unwillingness to give up or give in.

Take this person for example:

He was born into poverty and early in his life, his family was broke and were forced out of their home. He had to work as a child to support them. His mother passed away when he was only nine years old. By 22, he had started and failed in his own business. Shortly after that, he ran for public office and lost, then started a second business which failed within two years, on borrowed money.

A few years later, his fiancée died unexpectedly, and he suffered a complete nervous breakdown. Throughout his life, he lost eight separate elections, but in 1860, he was finally elected President of the United States of America. Who was he? Mr. Abraham Lincoln.

There is no question that Abraham Lincoln is one of the most revered leaders in all of American history. When you look at the record of his life, however, you'd be hard-pressed to believe in his greatness, up until the point that he successfully led his country through one of the most critical periods of its existence. What if he had given up? What if he had quit after his first business failed?

It's clear that Mr. Lincoln's failures did not define the altitude of his achievement. And this point is true for you too! It's one of the hardest lessons to learn and is critical to your success in life. You have the power to change. You have the power to make course corrections throughout your life and learn from the challenges that you encounter along your journey. You and only you can permit yourself to use that wisdom to move forward and make your mark on the world.

Growing up in an entrepreneurial environment and seeing this cycle of success and failure play out has led me to understand that it isn't a single defeat that can cause you to lose the game of life. Your success is based on your willingness to get up off the ground, dust yourself off and get yourself back in the game. You must understand that it's just part of the process and isn't unique to you.

In my own life, I've had to overcome a few colossal failures. I once started a real estate advertising technology firm that took off like a rocket ship. We had developed a novel new technology product that made a lot of sense in the marketplace and added a lot of value to the businesses of real estate agents, mortgage lenders and other real estate professionals who used our systems. We grew the company from zero, with no outside investment, to over 1 million dollars in sales and from 2 to 35 employees within 18 months. I thought we'd hit the big one, and I was only 33 years old at the time.

It felt like that entrepreneurial dream had come true. There were a lot of expenses, but the cash-flow was great, and it looked like we had made it! In fact, this was the first time in my life that I knew what it meant to have no money troubles at all. We were completely debt-free outside of the home and had plenty of reserves stashed away. We had more money than we knew what to do with it.

I wish I could tell you that the fairy tale lasted, the business continued to grow, and we rode off into the sunset with our bags of riches. It didn't. In the second winter, the business changed fast. The technology that our business was based on completely revolutionized within the two years we were in business and made a large part of what we delivered irrelevant. And the employees and overhead didn't slow down at the same rate as the revenue coming in.

They say that the larger a ship is, the longer it takes to slow it down or change its course. That is true in business. All of the sales revenue that we made in the run-up of the company had been reinvested, and the overhead started to eat us alive. We ended up closing the company at the three-year mark with hundreds of thousands of dollars of our personal investment lost.

Let me tell you something that hurt. I mean it physically hurt. I was crushed. I had poured three years of my life working up to 16 hours a day to make this dream come true. I had a serious case of self-doubt that I could ever make anything successful again. I mean, if you had something so powerful that took off so fast and made so much money while doing an incredible amount of good in the world and you lost it all, wouldn't you question your ability to make it happen again?

It took a couple of months to start feeling better after that failure, but the resilience that I learned back on the farm showed up, and I set my sights on the next chapter of my life. I got busy and came up with a new plan. I set out to reinvent myself. I had to pull myself and my family out of this financial wasteland. I went on over the next three years to have the highest personal income years in my entire career.

What would have happened if I'd just given up? Sure, I had a lot of reasons to lie on the couch and throw a big pity party. A lot of people would have understood why I wasn't achieving anything after seeing that huge "swing-and-a-miss." In fact, I had a few of them telling me that maybe I should just lie low, you know, get a safe and secure job and give up on those big dreams. But I knew, deep down in my heart, that the failure of that one business couldn't define who I was in the world and the value that I could continue to bring people in so many ways.

It's the same way for you too! No matter what trials and tribulations you've faced on your journey thus far, you can decide right here and now that you're going on to bigger and better things. You can set your sights on the pinnacle of your achievement and with commitment, hard work, and persistence, you can make those dreams turn into reality.

Most importantly, I want every one of you to know that you have everything it takes to achieve your goals. You have been given the most powerful computer, a sound operating system, and the most incredible architecture ever known on the face of the Earth since the day you were created. It's up to you to harness that power and make a decision to accomplish your goals.

Recently, as we were celebrating the New Year and looking forward to the great events and successes to come in the year ahead, I had a startling and somewhat chilling revelation. This was not just a new year; this was a new decade. A new decade! I realized that at the end of this decade, I would be nearing 50 years old, my children would be most of the way through their school years and off to college, and I would have come upon the time in my life that I had always dreamed of, being retired early and traveling the world. I gulped hard and felt my hands get a little clammy.

I got just a little bit anxious about what I would accomplish, starting off into this new era of my life.

There have been many times in my life that I was in this same position. It seems like the nervousness never quite goes away. That familiar dark, burning feeling in the pit of my stomach that begs the question "Mikel, are you up to the challenge?"

I made a decision right then that this decade would be the most productive era of my life and I would dedicate myself to plan and execute better than ever before. You see, that has been one of the most critical secrets to my success, and it's the same with every other successful person that I've ever met, listened to, or read about. The willingness to take the uneasiness and uncertainty of challenging circumstances and face them head-on is a hallmark of a true leader.

Napoleon Hill, one of the greatest thought leaders who ever lived, said it best "Whatever the mind can conceive and believe, the mind can achieve."

James Nesmith had a dream of improving his golf game – and he developed a unique method of achieving his goal. Until he devised this method, he was just your average weekend golfer, shooting in mid- to low-nineties. Then, for seven years, he completely quit the game. He never touched a club. He never set foot on a fairway.

Ironically, it was during this seven-year break from the game that he came up with his amazingly effective technique for improving his game – a technique we can all learn from. In fact, the first time he set foot on a golf course after his hiatus from the game, he shot an astonishing 74! He cut 20 strokes off his average without having swung a golf club in seven years! Unbelievable! Not only that, but his physical condition had deteriorated during those seven years.

What was his secret? Visualization. You see, Major Nesmith had spent those seven years as a prisoner of war in North Vietnam. During those seven years, he was imprisoned in a cage that was approximately four and one-half feet high and five feet long.

During almost the entire time, he was imprisoned, he saw no one, talked to no one and experienced no physical activity. During the first few months, he did virtually nothing but hope and prayed for his release. Then he realized he had to find some way to occupy his mind or he would lose his sanity and probably his life. That's when he learned the power of building his future in his mind's eye.

In his mind, he selected his favorite golf course and started playing golf. Every day, he played a full 18 holes at the legendary country club of his dreams. He experienced everything to the last detail. He saw himself dressed in his golfing clothes. He smelled the fragrance of the trees and the freshly trimmed grass. He experienced different weather conditions – windy spring days, overcast winter days, and sunny summer mornings.

In his imagination, every detail, the individual blades of grass, the trees, the singing birds, the scampering squirrels and the lay of the course became real.

He felt the grip of the club in his hands. He instructed himself as he practiced smoothing out his down-swing and the follow-through on his shot. Then he watched the ball arc down the exact center of the fairway, bounce a couple of times and roll to the exact spot he had selected, all in his mind.

In the real world, he was in no hurry. He had no place to go. So, in his mind, he took every step on his way to the ball, just as if he was physically on the course. It took him just as long as the imaginary time to play 18 holes as it would have taken in reality. Not a detail was omitted. Not once did he ever miss a shot, never a hook or a slice, never a missed putt.

Eighteen holes of golf every day, seven days a week for seven years. Twenty strokes off his score for a lifetime best score of 74.

Here is the question for all of us as we start our new decade:

What are you visualizing?

What do you have your mind focused on and where is that focus taking you?

Without a clear vision of where you are going, you're likely to get lost along the way. You may end up looking back at the beginning of 2020 wondering which road you took and how you arrived where you are.

It's your choice. It all comes down to a few simple planning steps and committed action on a daily basis in the direction of your dreams.

1. Fix in your mind the exact goal or desire in your life.
2. Determine exactly what you intend to give in return for the achievement of your goal.
3. Establish a definite date for the achievement of the goal.
4. Create a definite plan for carrying out your desire and begin at once, whether you are ready or not, to put this plan into action
5. Write a clear and concise statement including the exact goal, what you intend to give in return, the time limit for its

achievement and the plan through which you intend to succeed.

6. Read your written statement aloud for a minimum of twice daily, once immediately after arising in the morning, and once again immediately before retiring at night.

In closing, I'd like to leave you with two comments. The first of these is that your failures don't define you and can't defeat you unless you let them. Failure is simply a reflection point on your way to your ultimate destination. Failures are an opportunity to learn what to do better next time and to develop the wisdom that you'll need to impact the lives of many in a positive way.

Lastly, I want you to know that taking a step into the unknown on faith is purely courageous. If you have a desire to become more in the world, if you have a song in your heart that has not been released to the wind, if you have a blessing inside of you waiting to burst out showing your greatness to the world, then get moving. Don't waste a single moment worrying about what might happen if you fail. Do everything in your power to avoid failure but accept setbacks as part of the process of achieving your dreams.

And finally, a favorite quote from one of our cherished American leaders, Teddy Roosevelt, who reminds us that the person of action and determination is to be admired:

"It is not the critic who counts; not the man who points out how the strong man stumbles, or where the doer of deeds could have done them better. The credit belongs to the man who is actually in the arena, whose face is marred by dust and sweat and blood; who strives valiantly; who errs, who comes short again and again, because there is no effort without error and shortcoming; but who does actually strive to do the deeds; who knows great enthusiasms, the great devotions; who spends himself in a worthy cause; who at the best knows in the end the triumph of high achievement, and who at the worst, if he fails, at least fails while daring greatly, so that his place shall never be with those cold and timid souls who neither know victory nor defeat."

Biography

Mikel Erdman has been engaging and inspiring sales and marketing professionals for more than 15 years. A product of the success principles he teaches, Mikel started his entrepreneurial career immediately after graduating from college. He became a self-made millionaire at the age of 30. He has successfully started and grown multiple companies in the mortgage, technology, and advertising arenas.

Contact Information

Mikel Erdman
Goodyear, Arizona
(360) 450-3551
http://www.mikelerdman.com

Chapter 12
ENGINEER YOUR SUCCESS

By Julie Eversole

Most people consider Donald Trump to be a successful businessman. He has big dreams, big successes, and big failures, too. He started in business thinking big. While still in college, he made a $6 million profit on his first construction project. His net worth is currently reported to be about $2 billion.

He has had huge ups and downs along the way. Some of the companies he has owned have declared bankruptcy for hundreds of millions of dollars. And, yet, there are plenty of people willing to loan Donald Trump money because they believe in his ability to succeed. They know he will always get up again to fight another day. They believe him when he says he will never quit pursuing his dreams and goals. Because of that, he has achieved success and will continue to do so.

Most people don't work business deals as big as Donald Trump's. But, that doesn't mean they can't be successful. Success is personal and changes over time. To achieve success, we must set goals. Defining goals and dreams helps achieve success. The success you achieve is what you believe you can do. Therefore, we must believe completely that success, with all its ups and downs, is worth whatever struggle we encounter along the way.

Success is defined by each person based on their perspective at that point in their life. Success for you is what you define it to be. For example, someone may define success as earning one million dollars. But, another person may require much more or much less money to consider himself successful. Another person may define success as being able to stay home with their young or school-aged children, without having to work outside the home. Others may define success differently, such as with relationships or health. Perhaps, someone may consider himself successful because he weighs the same now as he did twenty years ago.

A more broadly recognized measure of success may be that most people believe someone with a professional degree, i.e., doctor, dentist, veterinarian, or lawyer is successful even without knowing their professional accomplishments. It's likely that some people may consider someone with a professional degree successful even as early as on their graduation day. This is because they recognize that even with no professional experience, recent graduates have accomplished something exceptional. This measure of success is typically just a milestone in a lifetime of accomplishments. Although most people would consider a new doctor a success, do you think the doctor would end his quest for success at this point? Most do not. Due to differing perspectives, some people may consider the professional a success long before the professional considers himself a success.

For most graduates, graduation is a milestone or the beginning of a quest for career or financial success. Someone who has just graduated, probably, would insist they have only taken the first step toward success. In reality, each step of our lives is a potential success marker. The pursuit of success continues our entire lives. Establishing goals and dreams throughout our lives helps achieve success. Celebrating their achievement leads to even greater success.

The most important key to success is to define success for you and establish and work toward goals to reach that success. Your success is up to you. To ensure success, everyone should set personal goals. When I was working on my bachelor's degree in engineering, I set a goal to graduate with honors. I researched the minimum Grade Point Average (GPA) needed to graduate with honors, and I graduated with exactly that GPA. I didn't have a single extra point to spare. I wonder what would have happened if I had set my sights higher! On the other hand, I know for sure that I wouldn't have graduated with honors if I had not calculated exactly what grade I needed in each course, and worked to earn those grades.

Goals should be specific, measurable, achievable, and relevant within a set timeframe. Goals should be written to make them real and to stay focused on them. Next, determine exactly what is required to reach that goal. This includes determining resources, timelines, and effort needed. Then, divide the tasks required into manageable steps which will culminate in goal achievement. People should have lifetime goals, mid-term goals, and short-term goals. The short-term and mid-term goals should logically lead to the achievement of the lifetime goals.

Let's say you want to save a million dollars by the time you retire in 35 years. To determine how to accomplish this, you need to break the goal into manageable chunks. Determine the amount needed each month to reach that goal. With a monthly investment of $435 at 8%, which is the average rate of return of the stock market for the past 81 years, you would have one million dollars in

35 years. Saving $435 per month, then, would become the short-term goal to ensure the overall goal of saving one million dollars is achieved. If desired, it could be broken down into weekly or even daily goals.

You cannot adopt anyone else's goals as your own. If you do, you cannot expect to be anything but mediocre. Have you known of anyone who became a lawyer, doctor, or teacher because that is what their parents wanted for them? In these cases, becoming a lawyer, doctor, or teacher often brings them no pleasure and little success. It should be obvious that if it weren't their dream or their passion, their heart would not be in it. Make your dreams your own. You have to define your dreams yourself and pursue them with passion.

I spent more than twenty years in the Air Force. I'm a retired Air Force engineer. Although I set and attained goals on the job, I never purposefully set personal goals while I was in the military. Specifically, I never strived to attain a certain rank. However, when I first entered the military as an enlisted person, I overheard another recruit say she wanted to become a Major because her father had retired as a Major. It should be no surprise that I retired as a Major. Apparently, I had subconsciously adopted her goal since I had set none of my own.

Without goals, you may be working on everything, and yet be heading nowhere. It is as though you are shooting at targets in a room, without knowing the location of the targets. Eventually, you might get lucky and hit one; however, the chances are slim that you will succeed without wasting precious time and resources. Additionally, how likely is it that you will hit the target you most want to reach? Success is much more attainable if you know where you are going and focus your time and resources on that target.

To help us achieve future goals, we should recognize and celebrate each success as it occurs. Each goal attained in our lives should be recognized and celebrated. When you've saved $435 per month for a year, or for ten years, celebrate it. When you graduate from high school, you should celebrate your achievement. When you've paid off your home mortgage, celebrate it. Although most people would like to have no mortgage, many people never set that as a goal, so they never achieve it. Your celebration of each success will result in positive feedback to you. As you see results from achieving short-term goals, you will be more inclined to set mid-term goals and believe that you can achieve them. This positive feedback about yourself will work to create a positive self-image in your brain. What you believe, you can achieve. For many of us, we need to reprogram our brains to truly believe we are capable of achieving our dreams. Also, we sometimes have to change our thinking to believe we deserve to reach our dreams. Allow yourself to fully consider and appreciate each achievement, and then strive to improve from there. Previous achievements make us believe that future achievement is possible. And for future success, we have to believe it is possible before it can become a reality.

Realize, too, that failure may be a necessary part of success. Consider Babe Ruth, the Baseball Hall of Famer. He held the Major League Baseball record for the most strikeouts at the same time that he held the record for the most home-runs. That may be because he always strived to hit a home-run. He was willing to attempt the best (a home-run) at the risk of failure (striking-out). However, it is unlikely that Babe Ruth looked at a strike-out as a failure. He probably just saw it as an inevitable aspect of making home-runs. Likewise, it is unlikely that anyone would consider him a failure in baseball even though he held the record for most strike-outs. Most likely, if Babe Ruth had been content with mediocrity, by going for a hit, rather than a home-run, we probably wouldn't even know his name today.

Our goals should include all aspects of our lives. Our lives need to be balanced in all areas, such as financial, spiritual, social/family, mental, physical, and emotional. What happiness will there be with success in one area of our life if it results in no time for anything else? Many people trade time for money; then they realize the desired success didn't bring them the happiness they expected. Specifically, someone may define success for themselves as earning a particular income. Once they succeed at earning that amount, sometimes they find out that they don't have time to enjoy the money or their personal lives suffered in the process. Perhaps they missed all of their children's childhood activities, or maybe their spouse left them due to lack of companionship. Strive for balance so the successes you achieve can be fully embraced and appreciated. This will ensure the success you achieve is worth the struggle.

Once you achieve your desired success, you should be prepared to incrementally improve upon that for the rest of your life. If you are content with where you are, you will not strive to improve and, therefore, you will not achieve excellence. Likewise, set new goals throughout your life. Don't let any success achieved be the best you ever do. Keep working to improve upon your achievements. Admittedly, the improvement or increase in success may be minute, but, continue to strive for excellence through incremental improvements. This will also be more likely to result in your keeping the success you have attained. Do this, and you will keep getting better and achieve more success.

Stay focused on your goals. For everything you do, ask yourself: Will this take me one step closer to reaching my goals, or will it take me away from my goals? If it does not help you with your goals, then consider not doing that activity. A major cause of unmet dreams is lack of focus. Keep your eye on the target. Every step you take should get you closer to your target, rather than farther from it.

There is a price to pay to achieve any worthy goal. Ensure you stay focused on the goal and how great the future will be once you achieve it. Never focus on the price to be paid. You can pay the price in tiny increments and reach the goal. You must be disciplined enough to do that. Keep in mind that simple disciplines repeated daily will help you achieve your goals. Also, know that problems will occur in anything worth doing. But, never let your problems grow to the point where they become bigger than your goal. Stay focused on the goal while you work out the solutions to the problems. Consider the problems to be challenges which will make you stronger, and which will make reaching the goal that much more fulfilling.

Make your goals lofty and what you truly desire. Donald Trump said, "If you're going to be thinking anyway, you might as well think big." Set your goals; then commit to reaching your goals. Never, ever, ever give up on your dreams! Never let there be any doubt about what you want: not in your mind, or in anyone else's. Once you have set your lifetime goals, don't ever give up on them, for if you do, you will certainly fail to reach them. The British abolitionist, Sir Thomas Foxwell Buxton, wrote, "With ordinary talent and extraordinary perseverance, all things are attainable." Perseverance is necessary to achieve anything worth having. Realize, it will not be easy to reach your goals; and if it is, you haven't set your goals high enough. Don't ever give up on your dreams and goals no matter how out-of-reach they seem. Success is not easy; but if you have set your goals on what you truly want, you will find a way to get there. Success is absolutely worth it.

BIOGRAPHY

Julie Eversole is an entrepreneur in travel, the largest industry in the world. She helps people achieve their personal and financial goals. As an Air Force engineer, she managed construction projects totaling nearly $1 billion in 15 countries. She oversaw reconstruction in war-torn Bosnia working for the Special Assistant to the President of the United States and for World Bank. After military retirement, she volunteered thousands of hours for her local school district, the Red Cross, and her church. For over ten years now, she has been a consultant to non-profit organizations. She has a Bachelor of Industrial Engineering degree from Georgia Tech, and a Master of Science in Systems Management from the University of Southern California.

CONTACT INFORMATION

Julie Eversole
9606 Limestone Pond, Suite 102
San Antonio Texas 78254

Chapter 13
BOUNCING BACK SUCCESSFULLY FROM ANY CIRCUMSTANCE

By Henry Maltez

How do you successfully bounce back to overcome the circumstances, challenges, and pitfalls of life?

Some of us may have gone through numerous difficulties in the past year. How do we release those thoughts that no longer serve and support us and others? No matter what happened, can we look at our circumstances with a renewed point of view? Is it possible that every situation that we experience is part of life's lessons and blessings that we are meant to learn and share? Can we continue to evolve with these lessons or gifts that we receive and use them to support and contribute to others?

With a new focus and appreciation, is it possible to return or "bounce back" with a new commitment to take the actions necessary to selflessly build the life and community we dream of?

For the purposes of this chapter, I am going to share two real-life accounts and some profound personal experiences, insights, and best practices that have supported me in having great personal and professional success this past year.

This story began on September 10, 2009, when I was informed that my mother was sick and possibly dying of cancer at a local hospital.

I had a very poor relationship with my mother, and we had not spoken for almost a year. I arrived at the hospital and spoke to her doctor to find out that she had stomach cancer and that it would be difficult to treat because it had spread to her liver. Also, she was fighting an infection that kept them from treating her pain and providing any possible treatments. The cancer could have been treated or slowed down if only she had sought treatment and dealt with the warning signs sooner.

I am sharing this as a reminder that life is short and that we need to honor and take care of our minds and bodies. My mother was barely retired after working most of her life. She was only 68 years old. My belief at the time was that she did not have much and that she had a rough life filled with hardship and sadness. I later realized that her legacy was so much more than I had ever given her credit for. My Mother was a strong Latina woman who could bounce back from anything. Whether it was money issues, poor health, failed relationships, or anything else, she always found a way to live her life joyfully no matter the circumstance.

Her greatest achievement was not only birthing, loving, and caring for her three sons, but having the will and strength to do whatever it took to raise her children as a single parent. I was the middle child and had a history of not getting along with my family and was always labeled a troublemaker.

After speaking with her doctor, the moment of truth came. Before stepping into my moms' hospital room, I found myself having second thoughts. I had several considerations about seeing her. Apart from the fact that our relationship is being strained and distant over the last few years, she told me that she never wanted to see me again the last time we spoke. However, something visceral inside me told me to see her, make amends, and love her as long as I could. I knew her future was uncertain, and I did not know how she would react when she saw me because of our history.

Committed to loving, forgiveness, and creating a new relationship with my family, I walked into the room with no regrets. Although she was surprised, her face lit up with joy. Tears and infectious smiles emerged from both of us, and I could see and feel the love she had for me with no regard for our past issues. I experienced a powerful lesson in forgiveness as we loved, laughed, talked and simply enjoyed our time together. We were completely present to the moment and were no longer conscious of our circumstances, past or future.

My mother passed away 12 days after we had reconnected on September 22, 2009. Although she had transitioned, her next great success came a few days after her passing when many of her friends and family came together to honor and celebrate her life. The lesson or point of view that I realized from this experience was that success is in the eye of the beholder. With approximately 7 billion people on the planet, success could simply be feeding your family. In this case, my mother's life was a success as she was honored for her contributions as an amazing human being. It was clear from everyone I spoke to that she had loved, supported, and profoundly impacted so many lives.

The passing of my mother was a difficult time for my estranged family and I. It would have been easier for me to carry around guilt and sadness and go back to my life. However, in the following weeks, a significant number of family and friends remained close and got together nightly to grieve, heal, pray, and remember her by sharing stories of her life. I believe we all found healing in our expressions of love for her. *"When I'm healed, I've not healed alone." - ACIM*

I truly believe the time we spent together enabled everyone to heal and bounce back successfully from the sadness of losing a loved one.

Simply put, the circumstance was that my mother passed away. We can choose the way we move forward and the experience we have as the result of any circumstance. For me, the blessings and lessons were that a loving family was brought back together to remember her and reconnect with each other to create new loving relationships.

Today, I found out that I have created an inveterate tendency to ask myself, what are the lessons and the blessings for every challenging or difficult circumstance that I encounter? Are my circumstances challenging or did I make them up? What is this situation here to teach me?

It is important for me to remember that facts are facts and that the only meaning of every situation is the one I attach to it.

Therefore, what I learned is that I could choose to be responsible for my own experiences and learn and grow from them. Life will continue to happen. It is up to me to generate the life, love, and success that I want for my family and me.

After missing three weeks of work, I returned to what I experienced as an uncomfortable and different environment.

At the time, I was a Senior Account Manager for a Fortune 500 company with the responsibility to maintain and grow a base of over 15 million dollars in company revenue.

I acknowledged that my job performance was affected by my lack of focus and my performance numbers were down significantly.

However, after 23 years of a successful track record, I truly believed I would quickly bounce back to create the results that I knew I was capable of achieving. After a few tough weeks of putting out fires, my immediate manager asked to meet with me and said that our Vice President of Sales would be joining us.

I clearly remembered the day, it was raining outside, and as I arrived for our meeting in a cold, large conference room, I could sense that something was not right.

I did not know what to expect, but I believed I was prepared for any circumstance. The Vice President immediately took control of the meeting and without any hesitation told me that I was being pulled out of my job and replaced. He was aware of my recent time off and told me that he was sorry for my loss. However, he and my manager felt that I needed a change. He shared some performance results with me, and I found myself quickly becoming defensive and emotional.

I knew I was turning things around, but it was not happening fast enough. The most hurtful moment came when the Vice President told me that this decision was made because I was not living up to my full potential and that I was being placed on a 90-day notice. I had 90 days to improve my performance, or I would be fired. After 23 years of loyalty and success, I felt my world collapsing all around me. This was my career and livelihood that fed my family, paid my bills, and put a roof over my head. With tears of anger, sadness, and regret, I attempted to challenge the decision with specific results and activities before sadly surrendering.

The Vice President walked out of the room to give me a few moments to calm down and talk to my manager. My manager was apologetic as she made me aware that it could have been worse and that I needed to do well in my new position.

The circumstance here was that I was being moved to a different position because I was underperforming. At the time, it was a huge blow to my ego, and I was extremely embarrassed. My experience was that the company I had worked so hard for had given up on me. I felt I was being judged by numbers and not as the valuable asset I believed I was. After many successful years of being a top performer, I had fallen to the bottom. My value to the organization had diminished, and I was now expendable.

I remember the feedback I received from the Vice President as if it happened yesterday. My interpretation was that I was no longer good enough and my ears could hear the echoes of his words "you are not living up to your full potential." Although the words were painful to hear, I later realized that it was the feedback that I needed at that time.

After a few minutes of talking to my manager, I began to experience a breakthrough and noticed a complete shift in my attitude. I immediately walked out of the conference room and approached the Vice President to apologize for being defensive and rude. I then thanked him for the new opportunity and committed to him that I would improve my performance and make him proud.

This could have been a challenging time for me as it was only three weeks since my mother had passed away. However, I knew in my heart that this was another opportunity to bounce back successfully from yet another circumstance.

Being responsible for my experience, I began to ask myself, what were the lessons here?

Was it to stay focused, work hard and never take anything for granted? What was the blessing here? Was it to be grateful that I still had a job in these tough economic times, or that I was given a second chance to prove myself?

What I learned was that I was responsible for my circumstances and that it was my actions that led me to this moment. The feedback was a blessing and a wake-up call to take inventory of where I was in my career and life, and how I would choose to grow and move forward. Life and careers will continue to happen. It is up to me to create the life, career, and success that I want to experience.

Another point of view is simply acknowledging that what I call my failures and mistakes are really lessons, blessings, and opportunities for growth.

This is where the irony of this story begins. I call it the unintentional, intentional result of wanting to step into my true passion. For the past few years, I was looking to change positions and even considered leaving a great paying job so that I could do something that I truly felt inspired to do for the rest of my career.

Although I had experienced success in sales, I wanted to contribute to the success of others. After taking some personal growth training courses including a train the trainer program, it was the art of teaching, training, and coaching others to be successful that became my true passion. Ironically, the position that I was being moved to was a sales coaching and training position.

I began my new position by coaching and training 14 sales representatives. Most of my new team were not meeting their sales plan and were considered underperforming. However, I was committed to their success and having them live up to their full potential no matter our circumstances. To accomplish this, I needed to support them by sharing the lessons that I had learned. The main lesson was to distinguish the experiences of self-perceived mistakes and failures from the actual facts of any circumstance. It was not easy for everyone to learn how to manage their experiences and surrender to the facts of what actually happened. After several months of observing, coaching, and providing feedback, my team was able to celebrate outstanding achievements, and several of them were promoted to be Account Managers.

As a result of my coaching performance, I was taken off of the 90-day notice within the first month of being in my new position. My ultimate satisfaction came from contributing to the success of others with no expectation of anything in return.

I was blessed to have this opportunity to be where I wanted to be and to do what I love. During this process, I was able to reinvent the perception that my management team had of me. The Vice President was very pleased with my results, and I was asked to take on a much bigger coaching role throughout our organization. Today, I can humbly and gratefully say that I am happy, passionate, and love what I do. It's okay to earn a large salary too.

Is it possible that we are already successful and just don't realize it because of our points of view?

Are you ready to step into your next level of growth and success? Remember your strengths, gifts, and how great you are.

Just when you think your life is spiraling out of control. A renewed point of view may reveal that your life is spiraling in control.

Circumstances, situations, considerations, events, setbacks, and rough patches only mean what you say they mean. They will continue to show up at critical times of your life. See the facts for what they truly are. It is up to you to choose how you experience the events in your life and to learn the lessons and blessings they are here to show you. Remember that you are not your circumstances and you have the resiliency and perseverance to work through them without ever compromising your well-being and who you truly are.

Life is full of limitless possibilities. The only limits that we have are the ones that we impose upon ourselves. If success is in the eye of the beholder, it is up to us to choose a successful and wonderful life.

Biography

Henry Maltez is a Sales Performance Coach with a passion for inspiring and contributing to the success of others. He holds a Master's Degree in Organizational Management and a Bachelor of Arts in Business Management. Henry has 24 years of experience in management, sales, and consulting at a Fortune 500 company. He also uses his strong leadership and experience to make a difference for others as a mentor, public speaker, trainer, and success coach.

Contact Information

Henry Maltez
54 Stoneybrook Avenue
San Francisco, CA. 94112
(415) 624-6000
henrymaltez@live.com

Chapter 14
LIVING INTREPIDLY

By Demi Karpouzos

For most of my adult life, I struggled to find my purpose. Sadly, I didn't know what I was passionate about. I'd stifled my emotions for so long, that I'd forgotten what brought me joy. Being the quintessential people pleaser, I was too busy trying to figure out what would make other people happy, to the extent that I didn't have time to discover what made me happy. Mediocrity was my status quo for the longest time. A camping trip with a friend set the stage for where I was, to end up because it gave me a glimpse of what I was capable of.

In high school, camping trips consisted of pulling the car up to the campsite, pitching a tent and sitting around the fire talking. So, when my friend Paul approached me to go on a 'real' camping trip where we would have to hike to our site, I accepted the challenge. This camping trip for me was a metaphor for life. I had begun with great excitement: some trepidation but more excitement. That morning, I threw together a few things I thought we would need on our trip. A few weeks prior, Paul asked if I had a backpack and I had told him that I did indeed have a backpack. The morning of the trip, when he came to pick me up, he looked incredulously at what I had slung over my shoulder. I discovered that a backpack and a knapsack are not the same. Not only had I thrown things together the morning of the trip, instead of properly preparing ahead of time but I made the grave error of not knowing what I didn't know. I was ill-prepared because I hadn't done my due-diligence, and this would prove to make our trip more arduous than what it needed to be.

We hiked for approximately 14 kilometers to get to our campsite. We were both exhausted. We pitched our tent, found a tree with a high branch to throw our food over so that bears wouldn't invade our site and I got ready for sleep. In the middle of the night, I was awakened by Paul yelling that the tent was flooded and we'd have to pack up and head back. It was 3 am, I was still exhausted, and it was raining.

The thought of having to hike back 14 kilometers in the dark and the pouring rain broke my spirit. I didn't know how I was going to make it. The first step was the hardest, but once we started moving, it wasn't so bad.

I would choose a tree or a rock in the distance to be my milestone marker. I broke it up into steps (a lot of steps). It seemed like we had been walking forever and I started to give up. It didn't look like we were nearing the end and I was tired, hungry, angry and wet. I didn't think I had another step left in me. Every time I wanted to give up, I remembered all the other times I had given up on myself, I didn't want to be this person anymore. And with this new resolve, I found out that I had another step in me and another and another. Before I knew it, I saw the truck, and I can tell you without any shame that it brought tears to my eyes.

Sure, I was exhausted, and I was now starting to feel a cold coming on, but the tears were not just tears of relief. My tears were for my epiphany. I was now becoming aware of how small I had been living my life because I didn't think I was worthy and I didn't think I had what it took to live a brilliant life. I now saw my accountability for the position that I found myself in, and I knew it didn't mean that I had to keep making the same choices. This small test of my will bolstered my confidence, and I was ready to test myself again. And I did! I quit smoking. I used the same method of making a promise to myself (or what some would call a goal), asking myself why I was making this promise, preparing and breaking it down into smaller steps. Initially, I broke it down minute by minute, and then when I had a little time under my belt, it became day by day, and at the 21-day mark, I knew I had begun to form a new habit. It was no longer a battle for an old way of thinking.

I wondered if this would work for purchasing my first home, real estate investment properties, stocks, or starting a business. I discovered that the answer was a resounding YES!

Lofty goals are great but beware of how you define success. I thought by earning a lot of money, driving a luxury car, and owning a condo on the lake, I'd feel successful. Don't get me wrong, I very much enjoyed what I had acquired but my job was just a job, and like most people, I dreaded Monday's and looked forward to Friday's.

Do what you love, take chances, live fully and when you can look back on your life, and you don't utter "I wish I had…," know that you have succeeded.

The single most important key to achieving success is persistent action. Thomas Edison 'failed' countless times with his inventions before achieving his desired result. But with persistent action, you must marry it with passion and knowledge.

What can you do to make persistent action part of your game plan? I challenge you to find what you're passionate about and then prepare by becoming as informed as you need to be to take the first step. Trust that opportunities will arise and people will show up when you need to take the next step. Abraham Lincoln said that if he had six hours to chop down a tree, he would spend the first hour sharpening his knife. That's all you need to do. Know what your goal is, why you want to achieve it, map it out, prepare for the first step and then take action!

You will probably encounter some roadblocks.

This is where a persistent action is crucial. Some of the roadblocks I've experienced on my journey have been self-doubt, insecurity, lack of self-worth and money identification. When making choices with this frame of mind, I soon discovered (well, not so soon) that the results were far from good and there was a distinct pattern that brought about my less than desirable outcomes. Because I was aware of my hurdles, I knew that I needed to take persistent action at every turn. I started devouring books.

I was relentless in my learning (and I still am), I read biographies for inspiration. I read self-help books to become more self-aware and do the inner work to re-write my internal dialogue where my limiting beliefs lived, and I read investment books to learn how to do what I wanted to do, to get to where I wanted to go. I attended seminars for motivation. However, I need to heed the warning here, for one not to become an information junkie.

I discovered that some people went from seminar to seminar and never took action or if they did take action, they'd allow their motivation to dwindle and then have to go to the next seminar to get hyped up again. Let this not be you. I saw some great progress in my life, but there were still a few trigger points I realized would keep me "stuck." As a result, I hired a coach. She not only held me accountable but more importantly, she was able to give me feedback from a different perspective.

For the first time, I saw where I was sabotaging myself and how to align my intentions and my actions. Hiring my own coach also helped me to squash any doubts I might have had regarding the value of my service as a coach. I understood that a good coach would get you to your goals quicker and more efficiently than if you try and do it on your own.

They say that we overestimate what we can do in a year and underestimate what we can do in 5 years. Remember that the time will go by regardless, so you might as well work toward something you love, and five years from now, you won't regret having done something different with yourself.

Lead your life, and regardless of what your position is in this world, you can be a great leader. A great leader will inspire people to do better and to be better. A great leader will do the things that most people aren't willing to do, even though they might not like doing it either. He/She has the discipline to do what's important. A great leader will consistently express their absolute best. A great leader will inspire and influence each person that he/she meets by their example. A great leader will treat everyone with respect, appreciation, and kindness, knowing that we are all connected and that when you give the best of yourself, you get the best out of others. Leadership isn't about dictatorship. It's about going out on a limb and inspiring others to do the same.

'Life begins at the end of your comfort zone." You need to trust that it isn't a coincidence that you're reading this book. You are hungry for something better, something greater. Take a chance. Live boldly. Get out of your comfort zone, and you'll realize what it feels like to be fully alive.

To get out of your comfort zone, it helps to find a mentor who has done the same. Napoleon Hills' book Think and Grow Rich has been a great inspiration for me. I am blessed because I have had several mentors in my life. I sought out people who were where I wanted to be. Some were several steps ahead of me, and some were years ahead. I found most of them in the books that lined my shelves. Find a mentor and remember that the only difference between you and them is just a step. Isn't it time you started living intrepidly?

Biography

Demi Karpouzos is a certified Success Coach. She has real estate investment certifications and has applied her knowledge to create a portfolio with several investment properties. She is a humanitarian and has had the great honor and pleasure of traveling to Africa on more than one occasion.

Contact Information

Demi Karpouzos
647-965-3364
demi@strategicalcoaching.com
www.strategicalcoaching.com

Chapter 15
INSPIRATION WHEN YOU LEAST EXPECT IT

By Brian Mahany

There is a picture on my refrigerator, a picture of a little boy. He is a little boy that I have never met, a boy with a bright smile even though he is suffering from an extremely rare and deadly cancer. Why is this picture on my refrigerator? Hopefully, by the end of this story, you will know the answer.

Although I have a large and beautiful home office, I frequently set up my laptop in the kitchen and work there. For many people, the kitchen is the "center" of their home. Across from the kitchen table stands the refrigerator. Like most other homes, our refrigerator does more than just keep food cold; it also serves as a message center and a place to display pictures, artwork, and magnets from trips taken long ago.

There are four pictures on my refrigerator. A Christmas family photo sent by a friend, one of my long-ago deceased family pet mastiff named Bear, a picture of my late father taken during World War II, and one of the little boy whose name I do not know.

Our world is filled with many people who struggle through life. They are everywhere. People living paycheck to paycheck. People struggling in dead-end jobs or failing relationships. You don't have to look far to find these people. Some only have to look in the mirror.

The sad reality is that a few will never find happiness or take advantage of a second chance in life. They will never see or seize the opportunities around them. From my days as a police officer and later as a prosecutor, I saw many failed lives. People who made the same mistakes repeatedly, who abandoned God or their higher power, who simply gave up hope or who turned to drugs, crime or alcohol as their sole salvation.

Thankfully, there are many people around us who make us smile, who motivate us to do better, who offer hope in uncertain times.

Fortunately for me, I have many successes in life. Career successes, financial freedom, travel, and a great family and friends. With all those successes, I should have no complaints. But few of us lead fairy tale lives. Misfortune happens to everyone at some point in his or her life. Disease strikes, businesses fail, relationships often hit rough spots.

Last year, my streak of good luck hit a rough patch. The firm I worked for fell on financially hard times and suddenly had to let some folks go. As the last hired, I was also the first fired. Ever the optimist, I looked at my sudden loss of work as an opportunity, a chance to start my own law firm.

Eagerly, I began ordering stationary, developing a website and scouting for new clients. What I did not anticipate were the thousands of other great lawyers that were also losing their jobs and a large number of recent law school grads that could not find any work in the field.

One very bright young lawyer I know found himself working as a part-time assistant zookeeper in charge of "cleaning up" after elephants and other large animals. Although happy to have a job, this certainly was not the career he signed up for when enrolling in law school three years earlier.

Just as these lawyers were struggling so was our new business. We happened to pick the worst economy in decades to hang out our shingle and start a business.

My earlier enthusiasm soon turned to fear. Without any money for advertising, how could we let clients know of our business and bring them to our door? How would we pay office rent? Our lack of income was beginning to weigh me down.

The legal profession was also changing. New lawyers facing tens of thousands of dollars of unpaid student loans were suddenly advertising rates so ridiculously low that we wondered if clients would even consider paying for our experience and hiring us.

Each day, the fear became worse. How much longer could I keep up with the mortgage? If suddenly finding myself unemployed at age 50 and struggling to start a new practice in the worst economy of my generation was not enough stress in my life, my beloved mother passed away.

With each passing day, the fear became worse; it turned into depression.

In November of 2010, one of my best friends called to ask for a favor. Would I accompany him to a fundraiser? I certainly was not thrilled with the idea, particularly with little money to contribute.

I attended more out of a sense of duty and did not know anything about the event other than the fact that one of our mutual friends organized it. Once there, I learned that the event was not simply a fundraiser. It was an event to celebrate the life of a young child suffering from a rare and virulent type of cancer. It was a way for the parents to give back to the community and say thanks. It was also an event to raise money for a charity that helps other families of children facing serious illness.

Not until I arrived did I learn how selfless the family was that threw this party. More importantly, not until I arrived did I realize that the little boy was the son of a mutual friend.

On my way to the event, I called my friend and pledged to stay for a few minutes of pleasantries then politely bow out. It was a Friday night after all, and I had plans to share a few cocktails with other friends at a sports bar and watch a game.

Throughout the cocktail hour, the little boy was running around the party. He ran from table to table surrounded by adults in jackets and dresses, this little boy. He was beaming, taking pictures and laughing. Surely, this could not be the boy who has cancer. He was probably the kid of some parents who couldn't find a babysitter that night.

As the dinner began, the lights were dimmed, and a media presentation began about the boy and his family. His doctors talked about the months of hospitalization, the pain, and the need for future care; his mother and father (both police officers) talked about their efforts to keep the family both solvent; and the family thanked the hundreds of caregivers, friends, and neighbors that rallied behind this little boy.

Fellow police officers and neighbors built a jungle gym in the backyard so the boy could play (he missed months of school and playgrounds). Local businesses helped grant the boy's wish to attend a Milwaukee Bucks basketball game (from the pictures, it looks like the team came through with front row seats).

This little boy who spent much of his life in the hospital and who faces a very uncertain future is the same little boy who was running around the hotel ballroom smiling and laughing.

Suddenly, my plans to "politely bow out" so I can have a beer with my friends seemed so unimportant. There would be many opportunities to go out on other nights. I had a great time that night and took home a photo of that little boy and placed it on my refrigerator.

The next morning while eating cereal, I began looking at the other pictures on my refrigerator. In particular, the one of my father, Lieutenant Howard Mahany of the U.S. Army Air Corps, proudly kneeling on the wing of his P-51 Mustang fighter plane. The plane displaying seven flags representing seven enemy aircraft destroyed.

That morning while looking at the photos on my refrigerator I learned two important lessons and returned to work on Monday with a renewed sense of energy and a much different perspective on life and work. Happily, I can say that since that morning, my fear is in check, my practice is doing very well, and again, I remember all those blessings that make me thankful for each day.

What are those two lessons learned that morning?

First, that life is precious. We need to embrace each day and the opportunities each day brings. Life is always going to throw curve balls now and then. Unfortunately, in these new economic times, people lose their jobs and homes every day. And despite many recent medical miracles, we all will die someday. The impossible odds faced by that young man suddenly put things in their proper perspective.

If we focus too much on our problems, we lose sight of the opportunities. That boy and his family could choose to focus on the pain, the bills, the lost childhood. Instead, they threw a party to thank everyone who helped them and to provide opportunities for other kids facing life-threatening illness. Don't ever try to tell that child he doesn't have the same opportunities as other kids. In some ways, he has more.

Without energy, inspiration, and motivation, life becomes more difficult. It's not enough to simply love your work. Success is inspired and sometimes that inspiration can be found in the strangest of places.

Obviously, inspiration is more than just a picture on the refrigerator. It's the realization that opportunity is everywhere if you look. I went to work on Monday that week and suddenly found all sorts of opportunities. I find my inspiration from great writers like Matt Morris, Timothy Ferriss, and their books. I find inspiration in church. And most of all, I find it through the stories of others, like the little boy on my refrigerator.

I said there were two lessons that next morning and wanted to address the other. They are equally important. The other photo on the fridge that provided me with renewed inspiration was that of my father. Dad was a fighter pilot and ace in World War II. In aerial combat, you survive by killing the enemy before he kills you. It's brutal but that simple.

Fortunately, life for most of us doesn't involve killing, but it does involve action. Anyone can spend his or her life planning, plotting and studying. The successful ones among us, however, are those that are also "doing."

Just like in combat, at some point, the planning has to stop and be replaced by action. Reading marketing books, hiring advertising consultants and developing detailed action plans have their place in any new business. No one should march into battle without a plan.

For many of us, however, we get so wrapped up in the planning that life passes us by before we take the opportunity to act.

As I said before, there are opportunities all around us. To enjoy them, however, we have to take chances and act. Our men and women in Iraq and Afghanistan take huge risks every day. Some pay the ultimate price in defense of our freedom and give their lives. The risks we take are usually not as deadly but to have any chance of success, we have to face our fears and take those risks.

What did I learn that day and the next morning? That life offers us inspiration in the most unusual places and that to succeed, we must not only be inspired but must also act decisively when opportunity knocks.

By the time this book is published, there will likely be new additions and changes to the outside of our refrigerator, but two photos will remain forever.

Biography

Brian Mahany is a lawyer with a national practice helping victims of fraud get back their hard-earned money. He also helps people and businesses with tax problems and those accused of white-collar crimes. A lawyer for 27 years, Brian previously served as Maine's revenue commissioner, as an assistant attorney general, and a criminal investigator. In 2008, he was part of the Wesley Snipes defense team. He lives in Milwaukee, Wisconsin.

Contact Information

Brian Mahany
(262) 970-8500
P.O. Box 511328, Milwaukee WI 53202
www.mahanyertl.com

Chapter 16
THE MONEY LINE

By Marc Accetta

I will never forget the first day I officially became an entrepreneur. I was so excited and filled with optimism. I drove down to the office where I would be conducting my new business, sauntered into my private office, and sat behind the new expensive executive desk I had just purchased to run my empire. I remember how important I felt. It was awesome.

I had a very small staff since most of the people generating income for me were independent, outside sales reps, so it was just myself and two other people. But that did not matter because they worked for me. I was their *boss*!

I spent the next several hours working my butt off. I made several phone calls to my sales reps to motivate them. I was working like crazy getting things around my office organized. I was amazed at how fast the day went. Before I knew it, everyone had gone home for the day, and I was still knee-deep in busy work.

The next day was quite similar to the first. The first several weeks were all quite similar. As my first month of business came to a close, I felt good about the fact that I had answered the bell and put in the hours needed to make my new business work. The only problem was that our overall company sales were terrible. Very few of my people were being productive. They were dropping the ball! I was very upset with them because I had been wearing my phone out "motivating" them.

I started to get nervous. I did not start my business in a traditional manner. I did not have a business plan. I thought that I could produce enough sales to justify going out on my own, so I did it. I started to realize that I would be short on numerous financial obligations that my new business had generated by the first of the next month.

I was panicking, and I was very angry with the unproductive people who were not getting the job done. I had set the office up perfectly. It was immaculate. All they had to do was sell the product, and everything would have been great. I knew that owning a business could be stressful, but I had not expected this kind of stress so quickly.

At the end of that first month, I had to get a loan from the bank to cover expenses. I had to get a girl I was dating to co-sign a loan so I could pay the bills. Something had to change and in a hurry. I was pretty certain this girl would not co-sign another loan the following month, and if I even asked her to do so, my possibilities of a long-term romance would be dead.

I started going back into blame game mode, thinking about everyone who was letting me down, and then it dawned on me that I should make sure that I was doing everything that I was supposed to be doing before I read them the riot act.

That was a wake-up call. I started to analyze everything I had accomplished that initial month and realized that even though I had outworked everyone, I had not been productive.

I had logged 10-12 hours each day. I was honestly exhausted, but I was not doing the high income generating activities that I had always done to be successful.

I thought since I was now an "entrepreneur" that I was a hot shot and I did not need to get my hands dirty. I would simply let "my people" do all the hard work, and I would get all the glory and a lot of the money. I was wrong.

I immediately learned the first lesson of jumping from an employee to an owner. The hours you put in are irrelevant. The ONLY thing that matters when you are the owner is the results. It doesn't matter how hard you try. The only thing that does matter is that you hit your numbers.

That was a radical shift for me. I will now have to come clean and admit that when I was working for someone else, there were days that I kind of went through the motions and "looked" like I was doing my job, when in reality, I was not. But on a job, we trade hours for dollars, so we get paid even if we do not hit the numbers.

Now I know that if you are unproductive on a job long enough, you will eventually get the boot, but it is not an immediate process. It can take months or even years before you pay the price for your lack of productivity.

When you are the owner, the only person you are cheating when you are not productive is yourself. I am very fortunate that I looked in the mirror and realized this so early in the game. If I had not, I would have been doomed to failure.

I did not do it intentionally. I did it because that's the way I had become programmed to work. Most people do not realize that our school system, while wonderful in many ways, programs us to be good employees. By the time we graduated from high school (or secondary school if you are from Europe), we had spent over 14,000 hours in the classroom. That's a lot of hours.

We all know the story of Pavlov and his dogs that he trained through classical conditioning to salivate when they heard the bell ring, assuming there would be food there. I don't know exactly how long that programming took, but I would imagine about a week. Can you imagine how classically conditioned we are after 14,000 hours? That's a lot of weeks.

We learn to show up on time. We learn to be well-behaved. We learn to do our work well and in a timely fashion. We learn that others need to be in control and set the schedule and agenda for us, and all we have to do is follow their orders. We get used to being graded and evaluated by our bosses (I mean teachers), etc.

Mostly we learn to watch the clock and put in the hours.

The problem is that we don't know what we don't know. So we don't even know that we were programmed to be an employee. To further compound the problem, where do we go to learn how to be a business owner? The truth is, it's uncommon knowledge. And to compound the problem one more time, this programming creates habits in us. We are all creatures of habit, right? And a habit is at least 1000 times more powerful than our willpower. Therefore, breaking our conditioning and creating the new right habits is a real challenge.

Most employees have a "What do I need to do?" mentality. They wait for their boss to tell them what is expected of them and then they normally will do that much and no more. That mindset will kill an entrepreneur.

So, with that information now in hand, I went back to work. The difference was that now I was not getting organized, or calling others to motivate them, now I started doing the highest income generating activities I knew how to do. The results were immediate and dramatic.

I had always been an outstanding salesperson. That is why I started my own business, so I went back to mission number one: Acquiring new customers.

Miraculously, at the end of the month, I generated enough revenue to pay all the bills and have a few bucks left over for myself. Not only that, my girlfriend was ecstatic.

So, let me ask you a few questions:
- Have you been confusing working hours focusing on results?
- Are you teachable and willing to learn how to break your old habits and learn how to think and act like a business owner?
- Do you know what your highest income generating activities are?

Almost every new entrepreneur admits that they have been feeling that putting in long hours is enough to get the job done.

You HAVE TO BE teachable to make it. You need to embrace the concept of being a lifelong learner. I have read hundreds of books on success and business principals since I started my first business. I have attended well over 100 live seminars too. I would say that I have easily eclipsed what I spent on my college education by attending business and personal development seminars.

The last question is the big one though. If you have not identified what your top income generating activities are, you will most likely not spend your prime business hours doing them.

At my live seminars, with my personal coaching clients, and on some of my advanced webinar series, I teach the concept of The Money Line.

It's very simple, yet very effective. First, let's identify what your prime income-generating hours are. If you are not sure, let me give you an example of what I mean.

My first job was doing in home sales. Virtually all of my sales calls were on weekdays from 6pm-9pm and on Saturday afternoons. How ridiculous would it have been if I was doing *anything* other than sales presentations during those critical, income-generating hours?

I had many other things that I had to do. I had to do paperwork. I had to make phone calls to set up the sales appointments. I had to train new sales reps. Before I knew this system, I would do those things whenever I wanted to. Once I learned how to maximize my peak income-earning hours, I only did those things outside *my prime earning hours*.

I have an attorney who owns his own firm and attended a couple of my live events. He ended up retaining me to do some personal coaching with him. The first thing I did with him was that I had him make a list of all the duties that he needs to do in any given week at his firm. Then we determined his peak income-generating hours.

Next, we decided on his highest income-generating activities. We quickly determined that he was delegating his highest income-generating activity to one of his employees because he was *too busy* to do it himself.

So, I had him go to his list and determine which things he had to DO himself. Then we determined what things he could DELEGATE to someone else, and finally we determined if there was anything he could all together DITCH.

With one simple adjustment, his business totally changed. He delegated the tasks that were preventing him from doing his highest income-generating activity and started doing that work himself, and he was free to do it throughout his peak earning hours.

For him, that work was doing the initial interview with a prospective client, which ultimately determined if they would retain him and become an actual paying client. His business went up about 400% the first year after he made that simple change.

Would you like to have your business grow by 400% this year?

Draw a line down the left side of your paper that goes from the top of the page to the bottom. That is your Money Line. Then draw three more identical lines (each about two inches to the right of the one before it).

Then list all your work activities down the left side of the Money Line. Once you have done that, then determine which ones you have to do, which you can delegate and which you can ditch. Next, take all the ones that you have to do yourself, and put them in either column 1 (must be done during peak hours), or column 2 (important to do in peak hours but not your highest priority), or column 3 (would be nice to do ASAP, but not during peak hours), or column 4 (could be done anytime).

Then prioritize doing everything that is in column one (right on the money line). If you have extra time to go on to the 2's and then the 3's, etc.

I know this may seem very elementary, but once you master this concept, you are well on your way to dramatically increasing productivity.

Do peak earning activities during peak earning hours and maximize the money line.

Biography

Marc Accetta has owned five successful businesses over the last 20 years including his primary company Marc Accetta Seminars. He has trained a million people all over the world in his live events. He has served on the board for his local Big Brothers Big Sisters for the last five years. He is also the Director of Training for World Ventures.

Contact Information

MarcAccetta.com
972.381.8675
MarcAccetta.com

Chapter 17
WHAT LEGACY ARE YOU GOING TO LEAVE BEHIND?

By Jill Nieman Picerno

When people think of what kind of legacy they would like to leave behind, they usually think financially. However, when I was a child, I knew that my legacy would be my children. I thought that the most important thing I could do for the world was to raise my children into becoming amazing adults. I always wanted to have two girls, sisters, as I never had a sister and always thought that would be so great. My wish did come true. I am blessed with two incredible girls. My first daughter, Jacquelyn, was born when I was 28 years old. Then two years and ten months later, Caitlyn was born. I was fortunate enough to become a Stay-At-Home Mom the day Jacquelyn was born, but this didn't just happen. My husband, at the time, and I worked very hard to pay off debts and make sure that his income would be able to provide for our family to live comfortably once I became a Stay-At-Home Mom.

I am also a CPA, and I started up my practice a little while after Jacquelyn was born. I ran my small practice from our home, which allowed me to continue being a Stay-At-Home Mom. I chose this career, while in college, specifically with this in mind. Parenting, not my CPA practice, would always be my number one job. I have read so many books about children and child raising, talked about my children and their various stages of development with my friends and family and even asked strangers their opinions about parenting. Once I began the parenting role, I set off towards creating my legacy. I knew that having an honest and completely open relationship with my girls when they were teenagers would be crucial to creating the legacy I wanted to leave behind.

Parenting is a tough job. It requires a ton of energy, and you need to realize how a parent shapes a child's future. We all want the best for our children, but sometimes, that gets lost in the day to day activities. We need to write down our goals for parenting. Look at how you were parented. What did you like about your parents' parenting styles and what is it that you don't like about their styles?

Many of us rarely take the time to sit down and think this through. Sit down right now and take out a sheet of paper. Let your mind go back in time and remember how your parents raised you. Write down everything that comes to your mind, without stopping, letting your mind flow. Keep writing until you believe you have captured your parents' parenting styles on paper. Now the fun begins. We are all creatures of habit, so many of us just parent as we were parented. That doesn't need to be the case. What type of parenting style do you want your children to experience? How do you want your children to feel about you and them? Remember to start creating your legacy with the end in mind.

Parents often ask me how I created such an honest and completely open relationship with my girls. Many things helped create our incredible relationships along the way, but there is one rule that I have had from the beginning of my parenting role. This rule, I believe, was the foundation of my relationships with my girls. My rule from the beginning was "No Lying."

Lying is always wrong. My girls learned at a very early age to speak the truth which was not a very easy task to accomplish. Children will lie to their parents. They lie to their parents to avoid being punished for something they did wrong in their parent's eyes. My girls did not like to be punished, like all children, but they did lie to me to avoid being punished. They soon figured out though that when they lied to me to avoid being punished, their punishment became ten times worse than if they had just told me the truth from the beginning.

They also learned that if they did tell me the truth right away about what they had done wrong, they wouldn't get in as much trouble as if I had caught them in the act. This was a little bit of a reward for telling the truth right away. Both my girls learned this rule and realized that telling the truth had its benefits.

Honesty is something their mother values. If my girls were not honest with me and lied, I would be very disappointed in them. Children do not want to disappoint their parents. Children just want to avoid getting punished. Parents should try to catch their children lying at an early age and instill in them the value of honesty.

Become a great detective. Learn the body signals that occur when someone is lying to you. Children will usually delay answering your initial questions. When they finally do answer your questions, their voice will have a slightly higher pitch to it. Their hands may cover their mouth or rub their nose often. Facial expressions will change. Their face may look paler and stiffer, their nostrils may flare, and their lips may look thinner and tighter. Avoiding direct eye contact, squinting or closing their eyes may also give them away. Their body may become stiffer, shoulders may be pulled up, and their elbows may be held close to their body. These are just a few of the body signals that parents may want to be on the lookout for.

Once you do know your child is lying, take action. Do not explain to them how you know they are lying. All they need to know is that you know they lied. Then tell them this is unacceptable. Explain to them the first punishment they were going to receive for having the inappropriate behavior. Then let them know that since they lied to you about what did happen, the punishment will be ten times the initial punishment they would have received.

Remember to have the punishment fit the inappropriate behavior, but make sure it is something you can and will follow through with. Your child also needs to realize that you were upset about their inappropriate behavior, but you are so much more disappointed in the fact that they felt the need to lie to you. Children lie to avoid punishment, but they do not want to disappoint you and lying creates disappointment.

When children start to reach the teenage years, this lying rule needs to be set in stone. You still need to be able to detect the body signals your child exposes to you when he/she is lying.

We must also realize that this age is a very difficult stage in your child's development. Try to remember how you felt or acted like as a teenager. Yes, that does scare some of us, and we don't want our children to make some of the same mistakes we did.

They do need to make some of their own mistakes, as they don't always learn from being told what to do and what not do. Being overly strict parents is not the course of action that seems to produce the best results related to some of their teenager's actions. I do believe this, as I know things about my female friends that their parents would not believe about their teenagers if I told them. Parents need to not parent with blinders on. The information I know about their friends becomes handy when trying to steer them towards a better path in life.

Teenagers are influenced by their friends more than their parents. You have to be one of their friends too. Always be the parent first and their friend second. Teenagers will not tell you that they like you being their parent and setting rules, but this honestly does make them feel loved. They know you care about what happens to them.

My girls think some of my rules are a little over the top, but they understand my reasoning behind my rules. They know they are loved. It's a fine line between having too many rules or too few rules or too strict rules or not strict enough rules. Hopefully, with this point, you have built that honest and completely open relationship with your children, as this will help guide you in setting your own rules for your teenagers.

This brings me to a question that has come up with my girls. Should I treat my girls the same related to the rules I have; yes and no. Yes, some rules should be the same, but every teenager is different. I remember having dinner with my girls one night, and Caitlyn began talking about one of her friends drinking her parent's alcohol. I asked

Caitlyn, "Which friend is that?" Caitlyn proceeded to tell me, in so many words, that it was none of my business and she didn't want me to tell her parents. I then explained to her that she did not need to tell me which friend of hers was doing this, but then she would suffer the consequences of my parenting rules being differently related to her than her sister.

Of course, life is not fair. I continued explaining to Caitlyn that Jacquelyn has told me many things about her friends and I haven't mentioned it to her friend's parents. My trust with Jacquelyn will be higher, and she will have more privileges related to hanging out with her friends than Caitlyn would. Needless to say, Caitlyn decided to tell me which friend of hers was drinking her parent's alcohol and we moved on from there. I have always kept my girl's secrets about their friends safe with me, except for one time. The only time I believe that I should tell another parent something about their teenager that my girls have shared with me in confidence is if it can be life-threatening. I got my daughter's permission to talk to the teenager's parents, as she was worried about her friend's life as well. Everything, fortunately, turned out great.

The teenage years are always interesting. I love that my girls feel so comfortable coming to me with any questions that they may have, but when the teenage years rolled around, their questions became life path altering.

Their questions became more about sex, drugs, boys, girls and so many other important topics about life in general.

Sometimes when one of my girls would come to ask me a question, inside, I am freaking out, but on the outside, I act as they asked me "What are we doing for dinner?" I was so proud of my girls being able to ask me any question they felt they wanted an answer about.

My girls realize that I don't know everything, but I told them we could always find out the answer together.

One question I remember one of my girls asking me was "Will you die if you have sex before you are 19 years old?" My daughter was just entering her teenage years, and one of her friend's moms had told her friend that. So began the talk about sex. I did tell her that "You do not die if you have sex before you are 19 years old." I think that the mother was trying to protect her daughter but didn't have an open relationship with her daughter to talk things out. This then led us into a conversation about AIDs, STDs, etc. The questions my girls came to ask were always a time to have discussions, and for me to steer them in the right direction. I realized that no one person can control another person. So I have tried to give my girls as much information as I thought necessary for them to make the correct choices in life. My girls and I are so glad we have this honest and completely open relationship. It hasn't always been easy, but it's always been worth it.

My life path continues today on creating a legacy for my incredible girls. This is how I measure success.

Biography

Jill Nieman Picerno is a very proud mother and entrepreneur. She is a student of parenting, finance, real estate and network marketing. She has thrust for knowledge, loves to meet new people, and visit new places around the world. She is a Certified Public Accountant, owns several real estate properties and has her own travel business, www.travelgirls.biz. She is also in the process of creating her very own parenting book.

Contact Information

Jill Nieman Picerno
10940 S Parker Rd, Ste 472
Parker,CO 80134
303-400-5100
jill@travelgirls.biz

www.ingramcontent.com/pod-product-compliance
Lightning Source LLC
Chambersburg PA
CBHW020639220526
45464CB00001B/215